Deterring and Investigating Attack

The Role of the FBI and CIA

Deterring and Investigating Attack

The Role of the FBI and CIA

Other titles in the Lucent Library of Homeland Security

Defending the Borders
Hunting Down the Terrorists
Responding to Attack
A Vulnerable America

THE
LUCENT
LIBRARY OF
HOMELAND
SECURITY

Deterring and Investigating Attack

The Role of the FBI and CIA

Jennifer Keeley

LUCENT
BOOKS®

THOMSON
™
GALE

San Diego • Detroit • New York • San Francisco • Cleveland • New Haven, Conn. • Waterville, Maine • London • Munich

LIBRARY OF CONGRESS CATALOGING-IN-PUBLICATION DATA

Keeley, Jennifer, 1974–
  Deterring and investigating attack : the role of the FBI and CIA / by Jennifer Keeley.
    v. cm. — (The Lucent library of homeland security)
Includes bibliographical references.
Contents: The terrorist threat—The technology to fight terrorism—Identifying suspects—
Following the money trail—Sounding the alarm.
  ISBN 1-59018-374-6
    1. Terrorism—United States—Prevention. 2. Terrorism—Government policy—United
States. 3. United States. Federal Bureau of Investigation. 4. United States. Central Intelligence
Agency. [1. Terrorism—prevention. 2. Terrorism—Government policy. 3. National security.
4. United States. Federal Bureau of Investigation. 5. United States. Central Intelligence
Agency.] I. Title. II. Series.
  HV6432.K44 2004
  363.32'0973—dc22
                                                                    2003015027

Printed in the United States of America

Contents

Foreword

S tunned by the terrorist attacks of September 11, 2001, millions of Americans clung to President George W. Bush's advice in a September 20 live broadcast speech to "live your lives, and hug your children." His soothing words made an indelible impression on people in need of comfort and paralyzed by fear. Recent history had seen no greater emotional flood than occurred in the days following September 11, as people were united by deep shock and grief and an instinctive need to feel safe.

Searching for safety, a panicked nation urged taking extreme and even absurd measures. Immediately after the attacks, it was suggested that all aircraft passengers be restrained for the duration of flights—better to restrict the movement of all than to risk allowing one dangerous passenger to act. After the attempted bombing of a flight from Paris to Atlanta in December 2001, one *New York Times* columnist even half-seriously suggested starting an airline called Naked Air—"where the only thing you wear is a seat belt." Although such acute fear and paranoia waned as the attacks slipped further into the past, a dulled but enduring desire to overhaul national security remained.

Creating the Department of Homeland Security was one way to allay citizens' panic and fear. Congress has allocated billions to secure the nation's infrastructure, bolster communication channels, and protect precious monuments against terrorist attack. Further funding has equipped emergency responders with state-of-the-art tools such as hazardous-material suits and networked communication systems. Improved databases and intelligence-gathering tools have extended the reach of intelligence agencies, in the effort to ferret out the terrorists hiding among us. Supporters of these programs praised the Bush administration for its attention to security lapses and agreed that in the post–September 11 world, only with tighter security could Americans go about their lives free of fear and reservation.

It did not take long, however, for the sense of national unity and purpose to splinter as people advanced countless ideas for actually achieving that security. As it became evident that ensuring safety meant curtailing Americans' freedom, the price of security became a hotly debated issue. With September 11 now years in the past, and after new wars and aggression waged in its name, it is not clear that the United States is any closer to becoming what many consider impossible: an America immune to attack. As distinguished political science professor Janice Gross Stein maintains, "Military preeminence, no matter how overwhelming, does not buy the United States security from attack, even in its heartland." Whether the invasion of sovereign nations, the deaths of thousands of civilians, and the continued endangerment of American troops have made the world any safer or the United States any less vulnerable to terror is unproved.

All Americans want to feel safe; beyond that basic agreement, however, commonality ends. Thus, how to ensure homeland security, and a myriad of related questions, is one of the most compelling and controversial issues in recent history. The books in this series explore this new chapter in history and examine its successes and challenges. Annotated bibliographies provide readers with ideas for further research, while fully documented primary and secondary source quotations enhance the text. Each book in the series carefully considers a different aspect of homeland security; together they provide students with a wealth of information as well as launching points for further study and discussion.

"We Didn't Know What We Knew"

On September 11, 2001, two hijacked jetliners hit the World Trade Center in New York City. A third plane crashed into the Pentagon just outside Washington, D.C., and a fourth crashed in Pennsylvania presumably en route to its target—most likely either the White House or Camp David (the U.S. presidential retreat in Maryland). It was obvious that someone, some group, had succeeded in organizing and executing a large-scale terrorist attack on U.S. soil. A country that had once seemed immune to such attacks was now clearly vulnerable, and the safety that many citizens felt within its borders was undermined.

In the aftermath of September 11, U.S. officials, lawmakers, and citizens alike found themselves grappling with the same question—how could this happen? A critical eye was turned toward the U.S. intelligence community, whose job it was to gather information about possible threats to the nation and its citizens. The media, the government, and the American public wondered why the intelligence community, supposedly one of the best in the world, had been clueless about the attack plans for September 11.

It quickly became apparent that the problem was not that the intelligence community had failed to gather information. In fact, it had collected a good deal of intelligence (and even distributed it to assorted U.S. government officials prior to the attack). Read in the proper light, some of this information may have alerted intelligence analysts to the possibility of an attack on U.S. soil. The problem, however, was that the intelligence community had failed to piece this information together and understand the significance of it. Bureaucracy, inadequate staffing, incompetence, and a lack of communication between agencies had severely hampered the intelligence community's ability to combine and share information. Without the proper systems to analyze information, the intelligence community fell victim to a situation that Robert Bryant, former deputy director of the Federal Bureau of Investigation (FBI), lamented: "We didn't know what we had," he said. "We didn't know what we knew."[1]

For example, on July 10, 2001, two months prior to the attacks, Ken Williams, an FBI agent in Phoenix, sent a memo to the counterterrorism division of FBI headquarters. This Phoenix Memo, as it came to be known after the attacks, warned officials of the agent's suspicions about a number of

Rescue workers carry an injured man from one of the towers of the World Trade Center in the aftermath of the September 11, 2001, terrorist attacks.

Some of the September 11 hijackers may have received pilot instruction at this flight school in Scottsdale, Arizona.

individuals attending flight school in Arizona. Williams believed that these men were al-Qaeda operatives backed by Osama bin Laden and were being trained to hijack planes. However, FBI officials viewed the memo as speculative and took no further action in the matter.

In addition to the Phoenix Memo, the FBI received a memo from a field agent in Minneapolis warning that a man named Zacarias Moussaoui might be the "type of person that could fly something into the World Trade Center."[2] Once again, the information slipped through the cracks and only resurfaced when Moussaoui became the first man arrested in connection with the September 11 attacks.

In addition to these specific memos, the testimony of a number of agents in various branches of the intelligence community pointed to significant information-sharing problems between organizations that hindered the tracking of suspected terrorists. For instance, in 1999 the Central Intelligence Agency (CIA) identified Khalid Almihdhar and Nawaf Alhazmi as possible al-Qaeda members. However, the CIA did not give this information to the FBI or local law enforcement agencies. Therefore, these two men were able to enter the United States, and since the CIA has no jurisdiction inside the United States, it could no longer legally monitor Almih-dhar or Alhazmi. Since the FBI did not know about the CIA's suspicions, there was no chance to monitor these two men in the United States. Almihdhar and Alhazmi lived in the country openly, getting jobs and driver's licenses, and went on to become two of the hijackers on September 11.

There is no way to know what information U.S. intelligence officials had or whether they would have been able to predict and/or thwart the attacks even if they had pieced it together. However, these incidents, in combination with other information the U.S. intelligence community had on al-Qaeda, suggest that it had severely underestimated the threat the organization posed. *Atlantic Monthly* correspondent David Brooks insightfully points out that a report produced less than a year before the attacks failed to mention the danger that groups such as al-Qaeda and their hatred of the United States posed. He writes, "In 2000 the CIA produced a report . . . in which it predicted what the world would be like during the next [fifteen years]. No, the report did not predict the events of September 11, and nobody blames it for that. But neither did it give any prominence to the atmosphere of hatred that produced September 11."[3]

Unable to go back and change what had happened, the CIA, FBI, and twelve other intelligence organizations that make up the U.S. intelligence community set about addressing the issues that led them to overlook important warning signs. With the CIA and FBI taking the lead, the U.S. intelligence community devoted a significant amount of its resources to investigating the September 11 attacks, tracking down those responsible, and bringing them to justice. It soon became apparent that this would not be its only task. The intelligence community was also asked to provide top-notch intelligence that would allow the U.S. government and military to predict and prevent future attacks. Thus, in the aftermath of one of the worst tragedies in U.S. history, it fell to the U.S. intelligence community to find any aspiring terrorists who might be hatching equally destructive plans.

Chapter One

A Unique Enemy

The terrorist attacks on the World Trade Center and the Pentagon dramatically demonstrated the destructive power that terrorist cells were capable of wielding on U.S. soil. Nearly three thousand people died and thousands were injured as the Twin Towers tumbled to the ground. Only one day in American history had seen the death of more U.S. citizens—the Civil War's Battle of Antietam on September 17, 1862.

The U.S. government, armed forces, and intelligence community had experience dealing with conventional terrorism, which typically involved the bombing of an embassy or another strategic location. Terrorist acts of this type sometimes resulted in the loss of hundreds of lives. However, the events of September 11 demonstrated the existence of an entirely new type of terrorism that killed thousands and destroyed skyscrapers instead of embassies. Before September 11, 2001, this kind of terrorism, called catastrophic terrorism, had existed only in fictional Hollywood movies and spy novels. As the planes hit the World Trade Center, catastrophic terrorism became a reality.

The U.S. intelligence community was charged with two important tasks in the days that followed: investigating the attack in an effort to find those responsible and developing tools and systems to predict and prevent future attacks. While such undertakings would be difficult under any circumstances, a number of characteristics, which were unique to terrorist cells such as the one that carried out the September 11 attacks, made the matter even more complicated.

The Location of al-Qaeda

As the investigation began, evidence indicated that a terrorist organization called al-Qaeda (the Base) was responsible. Founded in early 1988, al-Qaeda was led by the infamous Saudi-born terrorist Osama bin Laden. The organization initially drew its membership from the mujahideen, volunteer

The Empire State Building stands in the foreground as smoke billows from the World Trade Center just after the terrorist attack.

After the attacks, the New York transportation system was shut down. Here, people cross the Williamsburg Bridge on foot.

Muslim warriors who fought to defend fellow Muslims from the Soviet occupation of Afghanistan. More than thirty-five thousand mujahideen descended upon Afghanistan between 1982 and 1992 to fight in this jihad (righteous struggle or holy war).

The mujahideen were successful in their fight and the Soviets withdrew from Afghanistan in 1989. Bin Laden then turned his organization's attention to fighting the jihad in nations other than Afghanistan. The Gulf War and the U.S. military presence in the Saudi peninsula aroused strong anti-U.S. opinions in bin Laden. He was determined to use violence and terror against Americans at home and abroad in order to drive the United States out of the Middle East. U.S. officials suspect that al-Qaeda began to carry out anti-American terrorist attacks soon after its formation, including a bombing of the World Trade Center on February 26,

1993. However, locating al-Qaeda has proven to be far more difficult than tracking down more conventional enemies.

For one thing, al-Qaeda members are not contained within any one country, as conventional adversaries are. From the time of the creation of the Central Intelligence Agency (CIA) in 1947 until September 11, the agency's primary objective was to gather intelligence about adversarial nations, most notably the Soviet Union during the Cold War. While this enemy presented its own challenges, as author James Bramford points out, "There were some good things about the Soviet Union. . . . The first one was you always knew where it was."[4] The CIA could therefore point spy satellites and high-tech listening devices at the Soviet Union to intercept its communications and photograph its activities. Soviet activities were, for the most part, easy to detect by these means. The development of a new missile site, the creation of a new highway, or the movement of troops could be easily recognized in satellite surveillance photos. If the Soviet naval fleet left port to sail to Cuba, its movements were easily monitored by U.S. intelligence agencies. Also, the CIA always knew where

Mujahideen soldiers like these fought to end the Soviet occupation of Afghanistan. Osama bin Laden recruited mujahideen soldiers for his al-Qaeda terrorist organization.

the Soviet leaders were located (in the capital city of Moscow) and where to retaliate should America be attacked.

The same cannot be said of al-Qaeda. It is impossible to look at a map and point to a country ruled by al-Qaeda. Instead, al-Qaeda has a presence in more than fifty countries, including the United States, and this presence is quite difficult to detect because the organization relies on very small units of three to six people (called cells) that blend into society. "This civilian guise allows [al-Qaeda] members and cells to disappear into civilian life," writes Carl Conetta. This way they can "exploit channels of movement and communication not normally open to hostiles [agents from other nations that may wish to gather information about the United States or launch a secret attack]."[5]

Some of these cells are actually inactive "sleeper cells," composed of individuals who simply live as civilians in the country without carrying out any al-Qaeda business for months or years. It is therefore impossible for U.S. intelli-

The wife of a Pakistani man arrested for suspected ties to al-Qaeda displays his driver's license. Al-Qaeda has a presence in more than fifty countries.

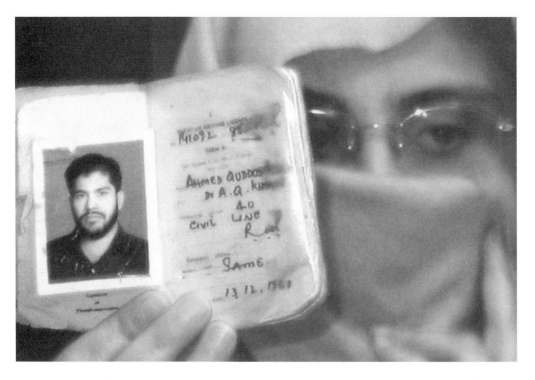

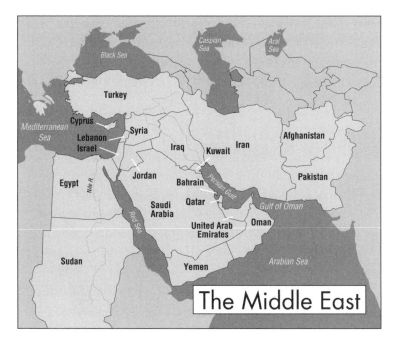

The Middle East

gence to find all sleeper cells or even to be aware they exist. Its members may lead normal lives as husbands, wives, and employees for many years before they are activated to carry out an act of terrorism against the United States.

Finding the location of the leadership of al-Qaeda has proven to be even more difficult than finding its members. The search for Osama bin Laden that began immediately after September 11 still had not located him by the summer of 2003. Unlike a president of an adversarial nation, bin Laden does not govern a specific country. There is no al-Qaeda presidential palace. He could be anywhere in the world. Locating all al-Qaeda members, and their elusive leader, presented a significant problem for the intelligence community after September 11.

Even if the U.S. intelligence community could locate the leadership of al-Qaeda, it is not certain that getting rid of Osama bin Laden and/or his generals would stop al-Qaeda from successfully mounting terrorist attacks against America and other nations. The structure of the organization makes it almost impossible to eliminate entirely. While some U.S. officials believe that getting rid of bin Laden and his generals would severely weaken the organization, many experts disagree. Abdel Bari Atwan, editor of the London-based *Al Quds* newspaper, argues that al-Qaeda would go forth even without its leader: "If Osama bin Laden is killed or captured, I don't think al-Qaeda will [be] finish[ed]."[6]

Wealth of Resources

Besides being hard to find, al-Qaeda is rich—another characteristic that helps it evade its enemies. In their report on terrorist financing, Maurice Greenberg and colleagues write, "Al-Qaeda differs from traditional, state-sponsored terrorist groups in one critical way: it is financially robust."[7] Indeed, the wealth of the organization creates a number of problems for the United States. Money gives al-Qaeda access to both destructive technology, such as state-of-the-art weaponry, and other tools, such as laptops, cell phones, encryption software, and Internet access, all of which it utilizes to achieve its ends.

Al-Qaeda's wealth comes from a number of sources, including donations from mosques and charitable organizations and profits from narcotics trafficking, kidnapping, and other illegal activities. A great deal of the organization's funding comes from bin Laden himself, who sources estimate inherited $300 million from his family before he was disowned. This wealth and al-Qaeda's access to it make the organization financially independent, unlike state-sponsored terrorists who must depend on funding from a government, or terrorist groups funded by just a few wealthy donors. Since al-Qaeda cells are privately supported, they can exist anywhere in the world. This fact led Greenberg and his fellow researchers and authors to conclude that the financial independence of al-Qaeda is "Osama bin Laden's foremost accomplishment."[8]

The Wrong Equipment

One of the most frustrating obstacles preventing the U.S. intelligence community from doing its job is having the wrong equipment. Although the CIA and the Federal Bureau of Investigation (FBI) have high-tech equipment like stealth planes and sensitive satellites, much of it is almost useless against terrorist cells. Ironically, they also lack some basic tools like computers, scanners, and e-mail that are critical for getting their job done. In fact, before September 11, "FBI agents were still using old '386' and '486' computers and had no Internet access or FBI e-mail addresses. After the attacks, FBI headquarters staff had to send photographs of the 19 hijackers to the 56 field offices by FedEx because they lacked scanners,"[9] writes journalist Chitra Ragavan. In other words, the U.S. intelligence community did not have access to the same technology that most American businesses, libraries, schools, and teenagers have at their disposal. Therefore, in the battle against terrorism, the intelligence community

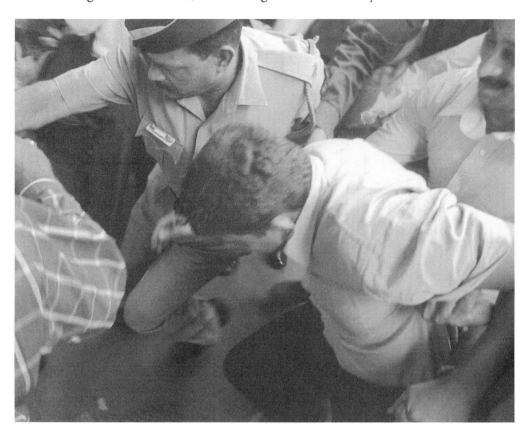

A suspected al-Qaeda member is taken into custody in India. Al-Qaeda uses state-of-the-art technology for planning and executing terrorist attacks around the world.

Fearing attacks on large targets like the Palo Verde nuclear plant, the FBI and CIA monitor the activity of terrorist cells. However, much of the surveillance equipment is useless with terrorist organizations.

started the fight with advanced technology that was useless against this particular enemy, and everyday tools that were inferior to those of al-Qaeda and other terrorist organizations.

This was the case because before September 11, the FBI and CIA had faced a very different kind of adversary. Therefore, they relied primarily on signals intelligence (SIGINT, information collected by intercepting communication signals of adversaries) and technological intelligence (TECHINT, information collected using high-tech technologies) to gather information on enemy nations. The CIA and the military intelligence agencies it oversees made revolutionary advances in these areas. Spy satellites equipped with state-of-the-art listening and photographic devices were very helpful in monitoring Iraq, Afghanistan, and other nations that U.S. officials believed to be dangerous.

Unfortunately, such devices were not very useful in the quest to monitor terrorists who adopt civilian disguises and whose whereabouts are unknown. Without knowing the al-Qaeda terrorists' location, it is impossible to point a satellite at them and listen in on their communications. As Dwayne Day, a leading authority on satellite technology, points out, members work hard to draw as little attention to themselves as possible. For instance, when the president of the United States travels down the street, he does so in a caravan of cars with a police escort. A satellite can easily spot this movement. Likewise, "the odds of catching Osama bin Laden with a spy satellite are excellent if he's driving around in a limousine with a big target painted on the roof," says Day. "If he's hiding, they're not going to see anything."[10] The U.S. intelligence community's inability to use these resources is the equivalent of having its best player on the bench.

While the U.S. intelligence community's advanced technologies did not make it much easier to find terrorists, the general availability of technology also became an obstacle as terrorists gained access to the same technologies that would be helpful to use against them. Fiber-optic lines, the Internet, and cell phones made it easier for terrorists to communicate anonymously, raise money, and gain access to essential information. Encryption software, designed to protect privacy and conceal identity, made it nearly impossible for code breakers to intercept and decrypt messages. Although such advances were great tools for e-businesses, banks, credit card companies, and other consumers, terrorists used them as well. "There is no one to blame for what is probably by far the greatest setback . . . to American capabilities for keeping tabs on terrorists," writes author Stephen Budiansky, "the fact that it is now virtually impossible to break the encrypted communication systems that PCs and the Internet have made available to everyone—including, apparently, al-Qaeda. The real culprits behind

Osama bin Laden continues to evade capture. Because bin Laden was trained by the CIA during the Soviet-Afghan War, he is familiar with the agency's monitoring methods.

this intelligence failing are the advance of technology and the laws of mathematics."[11]

Insight into U.S. Intelligence Practices

Another reason that conventional CIA monitoring methods do not work with terrorist cells is because terrorists are familiar with the systems being used. This is especially true in the case of al-Qaeda since it worked in partnership with the CIA against the Soviets in the Soviet-Afghan War. The

CIA trained mujahideen fighters (some argue that one of these fighters was Osama bin Laden) in espionage and stealth. In 1986 the CIA funded builders including bin Laden's construction company to build a tunnel complex in Pakistan under the mountains close to the Afghan border. Called the Khost tunnel complex, it was used as a medical facility and a training camp for mujahideen fighters. Finally, the CIA supplied the mujahideen with arms, including Stinger anti-aircraft missiles. Although a direct, overt tie between the CIA and bin Laden has not been found, it is clear that there was a great deal of interaction between the agency and the mujahideen that gives present-day al-Qaeda members insight into CIA methods and practices.

Inside Al Qaeda, the work of Sri Lankan scholar Rohan Gunaratna, explores the worldwide network of the terrorist group.

Al-Qaeda's training manual, a copy of which was found in Manchester, England, during the search of an al-Qaeda member's home, shows a good deal of knowledge about the methods employed by the U.S. intelligence community in its surveillance of suspects. For example, the manual's fifth lesson instructs its members how to communicate with each other without drawing the attention of security agencies like the CIA. Members are instructed to take a variety of precautions; they should, "select telephones that are less suspicious to the security apparatus and more difficult to monitor . . . periodically [examine] the telephone wire

INSIDE **AL QAEDA**
GLOBAL NETWORK OF TERROR

ROHAN GUNARATNA

and the receiver . . . telephone numbers should be memorized. . . . If a brother has to write them down, he should do so using a code so they do not appear to be telephone numbers ([like] figures from a shopping list, etc.)."[12]

Aside from this sort of training to communicate without attracting the attention of intelligence agencies, al-Qaeda has also shown the ability to discover what types of communication are being compromised and adapt quickly. "Bin Laden was able to determine that we knew he was using cell phones and satellite technology to communicate with his subordinates," says former Deputy U.S. Attorney General Eric Holder, "and once that info became public, he ceased to communicate with his co-workers in that way."[13]

The Problem with Good Old-Fashioned Espionage

Since monitoring al-Qaeda through technical means proved difficult, some experts suggest that the U.S. intelligence community should shift its focus back to good, old-fashioned espionage. Referred to as human intelligence (HUMINT), it involves the use of officers who pretend to be someone else in order to infiltrate organizations such as al-Qaeda. For instance, they may pretend to be wealthy donors or prospective members in order to recruit actual al-Qaeda members to spy for the CIA. However, penetrating a terrorist cell such as al-Qaeda through HUMINT presents a whole host of new problems for the CIA.

One of the main problems with employing HUMINT is that in the world of al-Qaeda, it is nearly impossible for a CIA case officer to establish a believable cover. *Cover* is a term used by intelligence officers to refer to a personality they develop in order to gain access to people who have access to information about the adversary. A CIA officer would not be very successful if he were to walk into an al-Qaeda training camp and announce that he was from the CIA and wanted information. However, he might be able to get information by pre-

tending to be someone else, say, a person eager to join the fight. This personality would be a cover, and in conventional espionage using a cover has proven to be a risky but profitable method of collecting information.

The problem the CIA faces in establishing cover when dealing with groups such as al-Qaeda, however, is overcoming a significant cultural barrier. For example, a blond-haired, blue-eyed, white-skinned, Christian American case officer would stick out like a sore thumb if he tried to join a group of dark-haired, dark-eyed, dark-skinned Muslim men. Ideally, the CIA would be able to send in a case officer who looked the part, possibly an officer of Arab descent. However, there are very few operatives from Middle Eastern backgrounds working for the CIA. Even if an operative looks the part, there is still a significant language barrier to overcome. The CIA and FBI both face a severe shortage of operatives

The CIA recruits Middle Eastern operatives, such as these Iraqi men, to help gather intelligence in places where the presence of American agents would arouse suspicion.

who are fluent in the languages—such as Arabic, Farsi, and Urdu—spoken in a number of dangerous states and organizations. A case officer also needs to have a fluid understanding of cultural mores and belief systems that may be foreign to him. As author Reuel Marc Gerecht puts it, "An officer who tries to go native, pretending to be a true-believing radical Muslim searching for brothers in the cause, will make a fool of himself quickly."[14]

As a former senior CIA operative suggests, the problem is that going undercover in such an environment is in many ways outside the realm of what case officers are willing to do. "The CIA probably doesn't have a single truly qualified Arabic-speaking officer of Middle Eastern background who can play a believable Muslim fundamentalist who would volunteer to spend years of his life with [bad] food and no women in the mountains of Afghanistan. . . . Most case offi-

A man wielding a knife runs though the crowd at an anti-American demonstration in Yemen. Anti-American sentiment is one of the biggest dangers CIA agents face overseas.

cers live in the suburbs of Virginia. We don't do that kind of thing." A younger case officer boils the problem down even further: "Operations that include diarrhea as a way of life don't happen."[15]

A "Holy" Cause

Even if the CIA could place a case officer inside al-Qaeda, it would still be extremely difficult to convince al-Qaeda members to work as agents because of the ideology of the group. Bin Laden and his followers are radical Muslims who believe that the actions of the U.S. government in the Middle East—specifically its occupation of Islamic holy lands on the Arabian Peninsula, its alliance with Israel, and its role in the Gulf War, which resulted in the death of thousands of Iraqis—are proof that Americans have declared war on Allah (the Supreme Being in Islam).

According to bin Laden, "Jihad [Holy War] is an individual duty if the enemy destroys the Muslim countries. . . . Nothing is more sacred than belief except repulsing an enemy who is attacking religion and life." Within this context, bin Laden challenges "every Muslim who believes in Allah and wishes to be rewarded [by entering heaven]" to do their religious duty, which bin Laden defines as "[complying] with Allah's order to kill the Americans and plunder their money wherever and whenever they find it."[16]

The conviction of al-Qaeda members that they are engaged in a jihad, that it is their duty to kill Americans, and that doing so will gain them entrance into heaven makes al-Qaeda very difficult for the CIA to infiltrate. Traditionally, CIA case officers have recruited agents within an organization through bribery, threats, and blackmail. However, it is unlikely that these methods will work on the average al-Qaeda member because followers fervently believe that they are fighting for a cause whose rewards are much greater. It is doubtful that people indoctrinated to hate Americans and the American way of life would want to assist the United

States in this way and still more unlikely that they could be enticed to cooperate through offers of financial reward, since they believe their cause is a holy one that will get them into heaven. Therefore, it is not likely that U.S. intelligence agencies will be able to get al-Qaeda members to defect from the group.

"The Best Way to Keep Silent"

In fact, al-Qaeda members' belief in the cause for which they fight runs so deep that many are willing to die for it. This willingness of members to die for the cause—including the willingness to launch suicide attacks—is another by-product of al-Qaeda's religious nature, and it makes the organization all the more lethal and difficult to penetrate.

That al-Qaeda members will die for their cause gives the organization many dangerous advantages. Suicide bombers need no high-tech, expensive, or complex system to deliver an attack. Rather than creating a device to fire a bomb from a safe distance, an al-Qaeda operative can deliver the bomb personally, driving right into the target city with it in a car and choosing the precise moment and location that will inflict the most damage. Another advantage of a suicide attack is that there is no one to track down and interrogate after the fact. The bomber is dead and therefore cannot be coerced or tortured into disclosing information about the organization.

Similarly, many al-Qaeda members who are not engaged in suicide attacks kill themselves just before the CIA can capture and interrogate them. In fact, many would rather die than risk falling into American hands, fearing that they may be forced or tricked into betraying al-Qaeda, their cause, their leader, and Allah. Journalists Paul Harris, John Hooper, and Ed Helmore write, "It was not torture or death [al-Qaeda warriors in Afghanistan] feared—the many suicides attested to that. Western defense officials believe they were afraid they would be forced to reveal the answer to the biggest secret

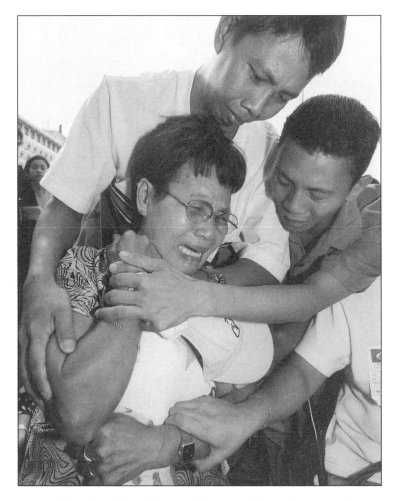

A Filipino woman grieves for her husband, killed in a suicide attack. Because most al-Qaeda members are unafraid to die for their cause, suicide bombings are a common form of terrorist attacks.

on earth—the whereabouts of Osama bin Laden. Death was the best way to keep silent."[17]

Openness of U.S. Culture

The openness of U.S. culture and the freedom of movement it allows also make terrorist organizations such as al-Qaeda difficult to fight since they take advantage of these vulnerabilities. Bill Harlow, the CIA's director of public affairs, told CNN, "In a country like ours, as open as we are, with the vulnerabilities that go with the freedoms that we have, it's very difficult to guard against all of those threats."[18] In other words, the very things that set the United States apart in the world—its openness, the freedoms enjoyed by its citizens, the freedoms enjoyed by visiting foreigners—also make it susceptible to attack by terrorist cells.

Protecting this vibrant, open culture in any era is indeed a difficult task. However, the events of September 11 vividly illustrate just how challenging this undertaking is in the twenty-first century. Stepping into a new millennium, the U.S. intelligence community has had to face off against terrorists with a diverse organization that spans the globe and has access to a wealth of resources. As a result, the CIA, FBI, and their counterparts are faced with a number of unique obstacles in dealing with this terrorist threat. And the days, months, and years that followed September 11, 2001, have tested their ability to overcome these barriers in order to find those responsible and prevent future attacks.

Chapter Two

Using Technology to Thwart Terrorism

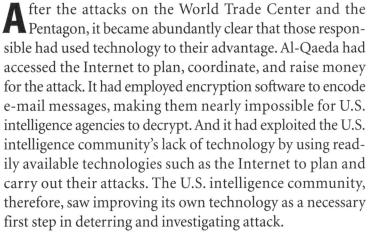

After the attacks on the World Trade Center and the Pentagon, it became abundantly clear that those responsible had used technology to their advantage. Al-Qaeda had accessed the Internet to plan, coordinate, and raise money for the attack. It had employed encryption software to encode e-mail messages, making them nearly impossible for U.S. intelligence agencies to decrypt. And it had exploited the U.S. intelligence community's lack of technology by using readily available technologies such as the Internet to plan and carry out their attacks. The U.S. intelligence community, therefore, saw improving its own technology as a necessary first step in deterring and investigating attack.

In fact, the need for technological solutions to help the intelligence community investigate and prevent attack led David J. Rothkopf, a former undersecretary of commerce, to argue that the war on terrorism would not be won by traditional soldiers. Instead, the United States would have to rely on some unlikely "war" heroes—"regiments of geeks ... pocket-protector brigades [that] live on rations of cold pizza and coffee. . . . The members of this fighting force are scientists and doctors, venture capitalists and corporate project managers—the private-sector army that is the United States' not-so-secret weapon and best hope." Said Rothkopf, "These unlikely warriors will provide the software, systems, and analytical resources that will enable the United States to track terrorists."[19]

Intercepting Communications

One valuable tool the U.S. intelligence community had in its arsenal to fight the war on terror was its ability to collect a great deal of data using state-of-the-art technology to intercept (although not necessarily decrypt) communications between terrorists. The National Security Agency (NSA) collected most of this information. The NSA is the arm of the intelligence community involved in communications intelligence, or gathering information by listening in on the (supposedly) private conversations of its adversaries.

The United States relies on its allies in the war on terrorism. Here, activists in India pledge their support to the American efforts.

The prize property of the NSA is ECHELON, a global surveillance system run by the United States, the United Kingdom, Australia, and New Zealand. ECHELON is a system of numerous clandestine listening posts around the world. Each of these sites intercepts e-mail, telephone, cell phone, fax, radio, and satellite transmissions within its range. The intercepted messages of billions of people around the globe are then fed into NSA supercomputers. Since the senders were not trying to protect their information, these messages are not encoded. The NSA computers can therefore easily search for any suspicious coded information. Amid the massive numbers of communications of virtually everyone on the planet who uses technology to communicate lie the intercepted communications of terrorists.

Once the U.S. intelligence community suspects that someone may be linked to a terrorist cell, that person's communications can be specifically targeted. The popularity of cell phones in countries where landlines are not readily available, like Pakistan or Afghanistan, has actually made it easier for the NSA and the Central Intelligence Agency (CIA) to eavesdrop and keep tabs on suspected and potential terrorists. Since the cell phone communications are bounced off satellites, it is relatively easy to find the potential terrorist's cell phone service provider's satellite, gain access to it, and intercept the communications without the terrorist ever knowing that the U.S. intelligence community is listening in. In this way, once the CIA and NSA target a potential terrorist, they can intercept her or his communications with fellow terrorists.

The Code Wars

Although the United States is able to intercept communications between members of terrorist cells, many of these communiqués are encrypted. Such computer programs make it difficult for the intelligence community to decrypt terrorist communications and use the information to successfully

The Menwith Hill Surveillance Center, in Yorkshire, England, is one of many surveillance sites in the global ECHELON system.

thwart terrorist plots. However, there are some methods and programs that are used to attempt to decode transmissions.

With the advent of the Internet, encryption software became readily and inexpensively available to consumers. E-mail encryption software that comes standard with most computers is called a PGP ("pretty good privacy") system. The average computer user can select from 2,048-bit or 4,096-bit encryption when sending e-mail. The higher the number, the more times the information is encrypted, and the longer it takes to try different combinations of data in order to break the code. At this time, it would take the world's fastest supercomputer billions upon billions of years to decrypt that message.

In response, researchers have attempted to build super-computers that can decrypt information. However, the only way to do so is to try every combination of numbers, symbols, and letters. In one such experiment in 1998, described by writer Stephen Budiansky, researchers "built a special-purpose computer that could test 92 billion different key sequences [of numbers, letters, and symbols] per second.... It took them fifty-six hours to break a message that [had roughly 900-bit encryption]."[20] While this was a significant triumph, the U.S. intelligence community still has a long way to go to be able to decrypt messages in a timely manner. Still, it continues to support research and technologies such as this, knowing that the ability to decode communications between terrorists would give it access to a great deal of information that would allow it to deter attacks and ferret out terrorist cells.

FBI and U.S. Customs agents remove evidence from the home of a man who allegedly created websites for a terrorist group.

Converting Information into Data

In order to hunt down terrorists and ward off their planned attacks, the intelligence community needs the ability not just to intercept communications, but also to wade through all the information collected and piece together relevant bits. As investigations into the September 11 attacks quickly revealed, the U.S. intelligence community's weakness was not in intercepting messages or gathering pertinent intelligence. In fact, some argue that it had collected the information it needed. For example, two months prior to the attack, an FBI agent in Phoenix sent a memo to Federal Bureau of Investigation (FBI) headquarters warning of suspicious individuals attending flight schools. He believed these men were training to be hijackers. Items such as this Phoenix Memo, along with warnings from the Minneapolis field office, and the CIA's knowledge that two of the hijackers were indeed dangerous were just the beginning of the list of information that was gathered by agencies before the attack.

The real problem was that, although the U.S. intelligence community had the technology to intercept and find the appropriate data, it did not have the technology to connect the dots, or sift through the data and make the proper connections. The Phoenix Memo on one FBI official's desk would have seemed more urgent had the official known about the existence of the warnings from the Minneapolis field office. Independently the two seemed like random information, but had they been pieced together, officials might have seen a pattern that would have alerted them to plans for the attack. Realizing that they would have had a better chance of thwarting the attacks if all the data they collected was organized, processed, and available to agents across the country, the CIA and the FBI began to fund software research that could help them process their intercepted communications and other information.

Since the first step in organizing data is getting it all into the same format, the intelligence community used cutting-edge software programs to put spoken and written communications in a variety of languages into the same format. One such software tool was speech recognition software. This software registers a word, parses it into ten- to twenty-millisecond sound samples that it understands, and then matches it to a database of words it is likely to be. The intelligence community found this software useful to convert the sounds of intercepted phone conversations into digital data (transcripts of these conversations) that could then be put into a massive database. To convert printed materials into the same digital data format that can be catalogued and searched, the intelligence community turned to optical character readers. Faxes are scanned by these programs and "read" so that printed text and characters can be transformed into data.

Once all of the data have been converted into a common digital format, it is necessary to convert them (once again) into a common language (the one preferred by the U.S. intelligence community is English). For this arduous task, the agencies used language translation programs that recognize words and sentence patterns in a given language and then suggest the most likely translation into English.

Data-Mining

Once the data are all in the same format and the same language, they must be sifted through. This is an enormous task. The amount of information collected by a global surveillance system such as ECHELON alone could not be monitored for suspicious content even if all of the personnel of all four nations worked around the clock every day of the year. And even if they could read every e-mail, translate every cell phone conversation, and listen to every radio station, the majority of communications would be useless to them—the conversations of everyday people about things such as taking the dog to the vet and e-mailing party invitations make up most of the communications intercepted by ECHELON. This information is useless in the hunt to find and deter terrorists.

The president of a data-mining service talks with a customer. Data-mining software sifts through intelligence to yield significant information.

Since it is impossible for intelligence officials to read every e-mail and listen to every conversation, the U.S. intelligence community employs software to do the job. Called data-mining software, these programs sift through the information collected after that information has been decoded (if possible), put in a digital format, and translated. Data-mining software programs employ a variety of techniques to look for patterns in all this information. In the case of conversations intercepted by ECHELON, the immense amount of data coming into the system is fed through dictionary software that searches for keywords and groups of words such as *assassinate*, *bomb*, and *Osama*. The words that the program searches for may be changed daily or hourly. As it sifts through the data it has collected, the software also looks for patterns, such as three e-mails between the same people in which the word *bomb* appears eight times.

Sorting through the enormous number of daily communications and trying to pluck out only those that pose a threat to the United States is a colossal undertaking, because data-mining software sifts through an incredible amount of information and divines similarities and patterns. Today it is used in a limited capacity, but the intelligence community is looking to software developers to improve it for future use.

The FBI's New Hardware

After the September 11 attacks, the FBI received a great deal of criticism for its lack of up-to-date technology. Experts argued that if the organization had developed a networked database (with or without data-mining capabilities), it could have assembled many of the clues that sat in piles on the desks of various agents. In the months that followed the attacks, the organization's technology was replaced with a new, networked database with extensive data-mining capabilities designed to assist the FBI in ferreting out potential terrorists and thwarting their operations.

To develop such a network the FBI hired Wilson Lowery, a former IBM executive, to manage a multimillion-dollar upgrade of the FBI's computer hardware and software. Lowery immediately understood how far behind the FBI's technology was and how difficult it would be to get the organization to catch up so it could compete with technologically advanced terrorists. He jokingly compared the challenge of upgrading the FBI's technology to the game of golf and "teeing off 200 yards behind Tiger Woods."[21]

Lowery contracted with DynCorp (one of the largest information technologies companies in the world) to provide the organization's new hardware—workstations, network cards, switches, routers, cabling, firewalls, etc.—and distributed more than twenty-two thousand new computers to the FBI's field offices. In so doing, he furnished these offices with technological capabilities, such as Internet access and e-mail, that most businesses have enjoyed for many years.

Lowery's new machines not only met higher standards for hard drive space, computer memory, and processor speeds, they also came equipped with Ethernet network cards capable of joining a TCP/IP (transmission control protocol/Internet protocol) network. (A protocol is one way computers communicate with each other. TCP/IP is the most commonly used protocol. In fact, it is TCP/IP that drives the Internet.) In January 2003, the FBI began deploying the wide area network (WAN) that will support these machines, connecting all fifty-six FBI field offices and giving them access to the same information. The new TCP/IP network will carry information significantly faster than the FBI's current network and allow agents at all locations to gain access to it.

The FBI's Trilogy Network

With new hardware in place, the FBI will release its new software package, Trilogy. Portions of it are already available to agents, and it should be completely functional in June 2004. The heart of the Trilogy package is a database called Virtual Case File, which was designed to track terrorists and criminals. The database will store up to a hundred terabytes of information drawn from state, local, and federal law enforcement agencies and the news media (one terabyte is 1,024 gigabytes—a hundred terabytes could hold the entire printed collection of the Library of Congress ten times). According to journalist Chitra Ragavan, Virtual Case File will also include a "40 million-page terrorism database of evidence dating back to the 1993 bombing of the World Trade Center, documents seized from Afghanistan, and 2 million pages of cable traffic."[22]

Virtual Case File will be considerably faster than the agency's previous software, Automated Case Support, which required users to scroll through up to eleven screens to search for information. The designers of Trilogy software also sought to make the database easy to use so that even the most technologically impaired agents would be able to enter data and

share information. *PC World* writer Elsa Wenzel explains some of the software's user-friendly features:

> Its search engine accepts natural-language queries. For example, when asked what could prevent future terrorist attacks, the database instantly found [the] Phoenix FBI memo about suspected terrorists taking flight lessons.... The system also draws maps and flow charts of the relationships between crime suspects. A search for hijacker Mohammed Atta, for example, yielded links from him to Osama bin Laden and dozens of other suspected criminals. Searches of foreign names and phrases will be easier because the database allows for a variety of spellings, according to FBI representatives demonstrating the new system.[23]

A New York police captain demonstrates a computer system that can access regional and federal law enforcement databases.

Lowery hopes that this user-friendly software deployed across a fast network that links all the FBI offices will help the agency sift through the massive amounts of data it collects.

TIA—Total Information Awareness and Terrorism Information Awareness

While the Trilogy network database is a significant undertaking, the hundred terabytes of information it is capable of storing are small in comparison to the Terrorism Information Awareness program (TIA, formerly called the Total Information Awareness program) of the Defense Advanced Research Projects Agency (DARPA). The program's goal, according to the DARPA website, "is to revolutionize the ability of the United States to detect, classify and identify foreign terrorists—and decipher their plans—and thereby enable the U.S. to take timely action to successfully preempt and defeat terrorist acts."[24] In order to achieve this end, DARPA proposed the creation of a database that would collate information from an unprecedented number of resources. The TIA program would combine each individual's credit card records, website visits, e-mail exchanges, employment history, medical records, banking transactions, and school and travel records into a searchable database. Pentagon spokeswoman Jan Walker explains the idea behind the database: "Terrorists

FBI director Robert Mueller is committed to providing his agents with the latest in computer technology to help track terrorists.

operate in shadowy networks. People have to move and plan before committing a terrorist act. Our hypothesis is their planning process has a signature."[25] If terrorist plots do have a "signature," then TIA will be able to detect the pattern using complicated mathematical equation and data-mining techniques.

TIA has come under fire from a number of sides. Civil liberties activists worry about possible abuses of the information, especially in the hands of an organization that is not accountable to the public. Meanwhile, software developers have reservations about the ability of software programs to use data-mining to track the activities of terrorists. While data-mining has become a valuable tool for retail businesses that wish to better understand customers' shopping habits, no one really knows whether it is capable of discovering a complex pattern of communication that could reveal a terrorist network. Paul Hawken, chairman of the information mapping software company Groxis, summed up this view succinctly when he told *Wired* magazine, "I don't know how you profile resentment and anger, but I don't think you do it from how many times someone goes to Wal-Mart."[26]

The War of the Web

While the U.S. intelligence community develops new technologies to identify terrorists and deter attacks, it also monitors existing technologies, like the Internet, thereby ensuring that they are not used to harmful ends. Al-Qaeda's technical savvy became readily apparent as investigators began to expose the planning for the September 11 attacks. It appears that al-Qaeda used the Web to solicit donations through websites purporting to be Islamic humanitarian charities; to recruit members by providing information about the cause as well as images, video clips, and contact information; and to gather information on targets, spread propaganda, and coordinate its attack through messages hidden on websites.

Many people like this
Internet consultant feel
that authorities should
not rely on computer
databases in the fight
against terrorism.

For example, analysts believe that al-Qaeda uses certain
phrases and symbols posted on its websites to direct its agents.
U.S. intelligence community personnel who monitor the sites
have noticed that "an icon of an AK-47 can appear next to a
photo of Osama bin Laden facing one direction one day, and
another direction the next. Colors of icons can change as well.
Messages can be hidden on pages inside sites with no links
to them, or placed openly in chat rooms. The messages and
patterns of symbols are given to analysts at the CIA and
National Security Agency to decipher."[27]

This use of Internet technology to plot and carry out terrorist acts has come to be called cyberterrorism, and experts in the area say that websites are the perfect way for a terrorist organization to communicate since they are much more difficult to trace than phone calls or e-mails. Consequently, "The Internet is being used as a 'cyberplanning' tool for terrorists," writes Lieutenant Colonel Timothy Thomas (retired), a military analyst. "It provides terrorists with anonymity, command control of resources, and a host of other measures to coordinate and integrate attack options."[28]

In an effort to hamper al-Qaeda's abilities to use the Internet to its advantage, the CIA and FBI surfed the Web in an attempt to locate sites being used by al-Qaeda to deliver messages and instructions to its followers. The intelligence organizations quickly found sites that were being used to convey messages. In one instance, "an intelligence-community analyst noticed something strange about a radical Islamist Web site she had been monitoring for several months. A

West Point cadets participate in exercises that focus on combatting cyberterrorism. Al-Qaeda uses the Internet to help plan terrorist attacks.

previously open, innocuous part of the site was suddenly blocked. She checked her notes, found the old address for the link, and typed it in—to find an otherwise empty page commanding in Arabic, MISSIONARIES ATTACK!"[29]

The CIA and FBI's Web-surfing efforts helped them identify a number of al-Qaeda–themed websites including www.alneda.com, which CIA officials claim contained encrypted information directing al-Qaeda members to more secure sites for instructions as well as general information. According to Ben Venzke, cyberterrorism expert and chief executive officer of the counterterrorism consulting firm IntelCenter, "Alneda.com is one of the only sites . . . for statements by al-Qaeda and the Taliban. . . . I expect it to reappear as quickly as it goes down and keep shifting."[30]

Internet Hide-and-Seek

The CIA's discovery of the site set off a battle of Internet hide-and-seek between the U.S. intelligence community and al-Qaeda members, supporters, and sympathizers. In this battle, U.S. intelligence officials locate the site, track down the Internet service provider (ISP), and have the site shut down only to see it reappear under a new domain name with a new host and a new Web address. In the beginning, the www.alneda.com site was registered in Singapore, but later showed up in Malaysia, where it was active until May 2002. When it was taken down at the request of the U.S. government, it reappeared in Texas at http://66.34.191.223 until June 13. When it was once again located by intelligence officials, it was taken down again. It reappeared in Michigan as www.drasat.com. All of the ISPs that hosted the site apparently knew nothing about its content.

This Internet hide-and-seek will no doubt continue, since it is likely that numerous al-Qaeda operatives have copied the site's contents onto CD-ROMs. This way, once the site is taken down, a different al-Qaeda member can sign up with an ISP anywhere in the world, upload the site, and spread the word about the site's new location through e-mail and other means.

Technology clearly plays an important role in the battle between the U.S. intelligence community and terrorist cells. It offers organizations such as the CIA and FBI promising tools to investigate the attacks on the World Trade Center and the Pentagon and prevent similar incidents from occurring. However, it also provides organizations such as al-Qaeda with tools to solicit donations, recruit members, and organize and plan attacks. Since September 11, the U.S. intelligence community in general and the FBI in particular have made incredible strides to procure the technologies most effective in fighting terrorism and hopefully nullify the terrorists' advantage in this area.

Chapter Three

Identifying Suspects and Tightening Security

The planes that were flown into the World Trade Center and the Pentagon did not strike just buildings, they struck at the sense of safety that many U.S. citizens had previously taken for granted. A number of the September 11 hijackers had lived for years in the United States as employees and community members. It therefore seemed that since al-Qaeda members could adopt civilian disguise, anyone and everyone could be a potential terrorist—passersby and neighbors alike.

In an effort to make citizens feel safe again, government officials promised to increase security measures around the country and to identify those responsible for the attacks (at home and abroad) and bring them to justice. The government said it would use new technologies and new methods both to prevent acts of terrorism and to identify other potential terrorists who might not have been involved in the attacks, but may be plotting future ones. In other words, it promised to find ways to identify terrorists before terrorists could commit acts of catastrophic terrorism. To accomplish these goals, leaders and lawmakers asked U.S. intelligence agencies to focus their resources on increasing security and identifying suspected and potential terrorists.

Beefing Up Security

The September 11 attacks shone a glaring spotlight on security weaknesses in public venues in the United States, particularly airports. In order to prevent further attacks, the Federal Bureau of Investigation (FBI) and the Central Intelligence Agency (CIA) looked into high-tech solutions to shore up these security weaknesses. First, the organizations focused on making certain that people who had access to secure areas in these venues could prove who they were—to make sure, for instance, that the airport janitor John Smith was really John Smith and not someone who had stolen his badge and used it to sneak into secure areas. Traditionally, photo IDs were used, but photos can easily be doctored and ID badges can be falsified.

The U.S. intelligence community looked for forms of identification that were more difficult to falsify. Since each human being has a unique genetic makeup—no two people's DNA is exactly the same—the agencies researched ways

Scanning of airline tickets can identify dangerous passengers before they board an airplane.

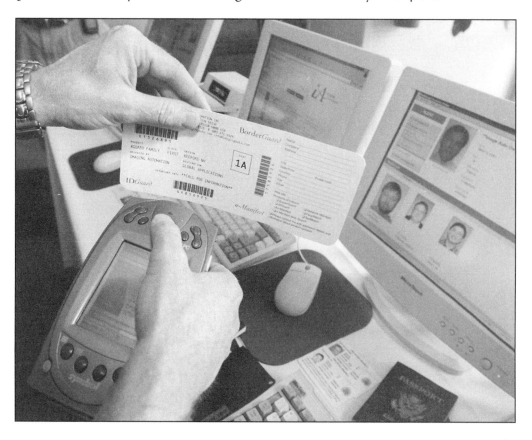

to use DNA to prove identity. Devices that aspire to do this are called biometric security devices, and they include face recognition technology, voiceprint recorders, fingerprint recorders, and iris scanners. These technologies rely on the fact that each individual's face, voiceprint, fingerprint, and iris are unique.

In the case of face recognition technology, "devices photograph people; break down their features into 'facial building elements'; convert these into numbers that, like fingerprints, uniquely identify individuals; and compare the results with those stored in a database," writer Charles Mann explains. "If someone's facial score matches that of a criminal in the database, the person is detained."[31] Face recognition technology has already been put into use at a number of public venues across the United States since September 11. For example,

Cameras scan faces in a crowd. Computers using face recognition software alert security agents to the presence of suspected criminals.

people who visit the Statue of Liberty now have their faces scanned.

While one day this type of technology may be able to pick random terrorists out of throngs of people, it is not yet advanced enough to handle this task. In a recent test of a face recognition system at a Florida airport, the device could not consistently recognize the faces of fifteen employees it was supposed to "know." It failed almost half the time and was easily fooled by glasses or quick head movements. This led one civil liberties expert to remark, "The facts show that under real-world conditions, Osama bin Laden himself could easily evade a face recognition system."[32]

There are other biometric devices available, such as iris scanners and fingerprint recorders. These devices store a database of digital pictures of the irises or fingerprints of authorized personnel. To check a person's identity, the device scans the iris or the fingerprint of the person who wishes to gain entry to a secured area, using either a light sensor system similar to that used in digital cameras (optical scanners) or an electrical current (capacitance scanners). Once the machine has an image of the person's iris or fingerprint, it compares this image to those stored in the authorized database. If there is a match, the person is allowed to pass.

However, iris scanners and fingerprint recorders have also proven easy to evade in real-world situations. Optical scanners cannot always tell the difference between a picture of a finger and a real one, and capacitance scanners can be fooled by a crafty contact lens or finger mold. Still, U.S. intelligence agencies support research to further develop these technologies in the hopes that they will one day be able to accurately identify a terrorist who is trying to breach a secured area.

The CIA's Hunt for al-Qaeda Abroad

While tightening security at home, the intelligence community also began the process of identifying al-Qaeda suspects

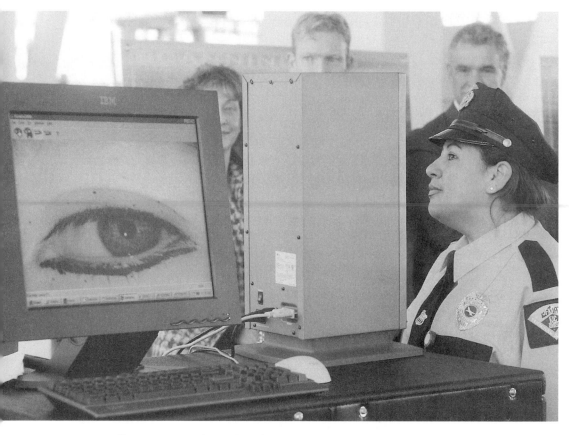

A security officer at New York's JFK Airport is identified by an iris scanner. Iris scanners are biometric devices used to prevent security breaches.

abroad and dismantling the organization in the weeks after September 11. To do this, the CIA developed a top secret "Worldwide Attack Matrix," which outlined a clandestine antiterrorism campaign that included covert actions in eighty countries around the world. This highly classified plan details action programs ranging from propaganda operations to the extermination of terrorist groups and individuals. President Bush approved this plan and also signed a general intelligence order that gave the organization unprecedented power to carry out operations (including assassinations) without first asking for presidential approval. CIA director George Tenet also argued that the agency should play a significant role in Afghanistan. On September 27, 2001, the members of a secret CIA unit called the Special Activities Division arrived in Afghanistan to search for bin Laden and al-Qaeda. The unit consisted of roughly 150 members—fighters, pilots, and specialists in a variety of areas. The division was equipped with helicopters, airplanes, unmanned aerial Predator drones with high-resolution cameras, and Hellfire antitank missiles.

The CIA secret unit was charged with finding al-Qaeda members (most notably bin Laden) and either capturing them or reporting their strategic location(s) back to the U.S. military in preparation for air or ground strikes. While CIA Predators prowled Afghanistan looking for troops, analysts at the CIA's counterterrorism center (CTC) back in the United States sorted through cell phone records to match names to calls and recipients. They also examined satellite photos for the slightest sign of al-Qaeda and scrutinized intercepted electronic communications. In addition, analysts sorted

Battle-training and flight-simulation software are becoming more advanced in order to better train military personnel.

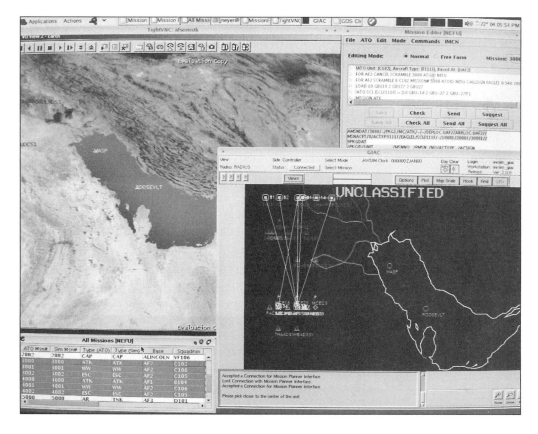

through thousands of communications from CIA field offices and information about al-Qaeda gathered by the intelligence agencies of other nations in the last decade.

When precision bombing forced al-Qaeda leaders to flee their strongholds in Afghanistan, they left behind a great deal of detailed information, which helped U.S. officials put names to faces of some of the world's most elusive terrorists. Suddenly CIA analysts had access to al-Qaeda members' address books, financial records, computers, and videos. Journalist David Kaplan details some intelligence treasures the CIA found:

> Among the key finds: rosters of trainees at al Qaeda facilities, which gave the CIA a handle on the tens of thousands of jihadists [al-Qaeda warriors] who had passed through some 50 camps across Afghanistan.
>
> Investigators also found in the rubble [of a November attack] scores of documents and videotapes that would spark alerts in a half-dozen countries. The videos featured five would-be martyrs railing against "infidels" and vowing to die in suicide attacks. Analysts soon recognized one of them: 30-year-old Ramzi Binalshibh . . . [and captured him] in Pakistan months later.
>
> From the rubble came another video, one revealing assassination plots against leaders at an upcoming Persian Gulf summit. U.S. officials pulled faces off the tape of some 45 al Qaeda operatives. . . . But perhaps the biggest find was yet another video—a homemade, 20-minute surveillance tape of [sites in] Singapore. The tape helped officials there thwart an extraordinary series of plots by Jamaat Islamiya—al Qaeda's key ally in Southeast Asia.[33]

Each successful strike yielded new intelligence, which allowed CIA analysts back in the United States to identify and set about capturing still more suspected terrorists throughout the world.

The New FBI

While the CIA used its resources to ferret out al-Qaeda and other potential terrorist groups abroad, the FBI worked on revamping itself to do the same at home. Until September 11, the FBI's mission was to investigate crimes that had already occurred and catch the criminals responsible. After the attacks, however, its focus broadened from simply investigating attacks to deterring them as well. White House chief of staff Andrew Card explained how the FBI's mandate changed with one sentence uttered by President George W. Bush a few days after September 11: "The president said, 'What are you doing to prevent the next attack?' That was a change in mind-set that the president introduced."[34] With those words, Bush changed the FBI from an agency with the mission of investigating crime to one that sought to prevent crime, specifically terrorism. This change led former U.S. attorney Loretta Lynch to remark, "We are experiencing a switch in the law enforcement paradigm in this country. It primarily was reactive. . . . [Now] we are really switching into a deterrence mode. The nature of the threat requires that we try and actually prevent actions before they occur."[35]

As of June 2002 counterterrorism became the FBI's top priority. FBI director Robert S. Mueller made changes in the FBI workforce to bring it in line with its new focus. He shifted five hundred agents from drug squads to counterterrorism work. He also tried to diversify the FBI staff, which was largely made up of white men who would have difficulty penetrating American Arab society. After September 11 the FBI hired three hundred language translaters who were fluent in Arabic, Farsi, Urdu, and other languages spoken in a number of dangerous states and organizations. Still, as of summer 2003, the agency had only seventy-six field agents who spoke Arabic, the language that al-Qaeda members use.

Mueller had plans to hire an additional seven hundred intelligence analysts to relieve the burden placed on already overworked agents and to further increase the diversity of

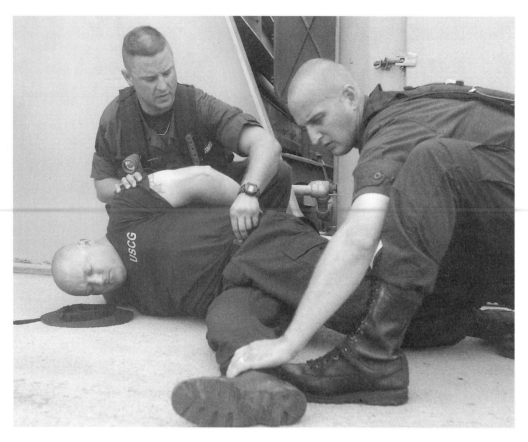

The FBI's principal focus has shifted from investigating criminal activity to preventing terrorist activity. Here, agents subdue a suspected terrorist during a drill.

the FBI workforce. Ironically, however, tight security checks have stifled his plans. On the one hand, the individuals the FBI needs to hire must speak Arabic and have ties to the Middle East—the FBI sees these ties as a potential security threat, and so it is difficult to get these individuals hired. Because most Arab Americans have ties to the Middle East, very few people can meet these stringent security standards, which are slow to change in the huge bureaucracy of the FBI.

In addition to these changes in personnel, the FBI has mandated a change in attitude. Director Mueller has asked his agents to increase their vigilance in order to identify suspected terrorists. For example, FBI agents are now expected to follow up every lead just in case it may lead them to a terrorist. According to one FBI official, this is a significant change and one not welcomed by all agents: "You used to look at threats; you knew what had validity; you'd get to them after you got all these other things out of the way.... Now, no matter how bizarre or how routine, you go after them."[36] While agents may grumble at the new system and the increased workload it creates, Mueller maintains that "the possibility of that lead, if that lead were followed, identifying somebody who wanted to kill Americans"[37] is worth the extra effort.

Ferreting Out Suspected Terrorists at Home

By following leads and cultivating sources, the FBI works to find al-Qaeda members who conspired with the September 11 hijackers as well as other terrorists (members of al-Qaeda or of other groups) who may be hatching plans to harm Americans. One of the most common ways to identify potential terrorists is surveillance and communications monitoring.

Through the use of data-mining systems, the FBI can now examine e-mail and Internet chat rooms for suspicious behaviors. In addition, the FBI now has access to library records to keep track of Internet usage and what kinds of books are being checked out in libraries across the country. Ideally, if someone were checking out books on the construction of a high-profile building, or how to make homemade bombs, this person would be flagged by the FBI. In a nationwide survey of fifteen hundred libraries conducted in December 2001, roughly 15 percent had received information requests from the FBI.

Financial transactions are also under surveillance by FBI agents. Tracking people's purchases allows the FBI to observe consumers' buying habits. If some terrorist organization is purchasing the tools to build some sort of weapon or hatch some sort of plan, the FBI hopes to notice the pattern of these transactions and be able to thwart the plan before it is put into action.

Once the FBI has a suspect or a suspicious organization in its sights, it begins to collect intelligence on the subject. The FBI can gather basic information about the person's home, marital status, citizenship, job status, and religious and political affiliations simply by searching a variety of databases and a number of Internet sites. An FBI agent might also ask informants (people who give information to law enforcement officials in exchange for money or favors) about the suspect. Finally, the FBI can examine the suspect's medical, financial, educational, and library records for any unusual patterns. For instance, the FBI might examine a suspect's financial records to see if he or she donates to charities that are known to be linked to al-Qaeda. Or investigators may examine the suspect's pharmaceutical purchases and see that massive quantities of antibiotics were purchased, piquing investigators' curiosity as to why someone would be stockpiling such a thing.

In addition to gathering intelligence, the FBI might also put a subject under surveillance, that is, keep a close watch on someone. Photo surveillance involves an officer using photographic equipment such as cameras and video to secretly film or take pictures of a suspect from afar. Or it can involve the deployment of hidden cameras to monitor the suspect at all

Due to effective surveillance, authorities apprehended these six men who were allegedly part of an al-Qaeda cell.

times. Surveillance can also include the installation of a telephone or computer wiretap, which allows FBI officers to listen in on the suspect's conversations and/or gain access to online communications and computer files. In some cases, the FBI can also obtain a warrant to search a suspect's voice mail.

USA Patriot Act

The methods available to the FBI to ferret out and monitor potential terrorists changed greatly after September 11 due to the passage of the USA Patriot Act in October 2001. The name is an acronym that stands for Uniting and Strengthening America by Providing Appropriate Tools Required to Intercept and Obstruct Terrorism. The passage of the act granted the FBI expanded surveillance authority that lowered the amount of evidence necessary to obtain wiretaps and search warrants, and even made them unnecessary to obtain in some situations. The Patriot Act granted the organization easier access to an individual's financial, medical, and library records. It also allowed the FBI to monitor individual citizens' Internet habits by requesting information about websites visited from ISPs and monitoring chat rooms and e-mail. In collaboration with government officials such as Attorney General John

Activists protest the USA Patriot Act in 2003. Many believe the new laws violate constitutional rights to privacy and freedom.

Ashcroft, the FBI argued forcefully that it needed these expanded powers to identify and apprehend suspected terrorists.

The act has faced a great deal of criticism from all sides since its passage. More than a hundred U.S. cities have passed resolutions protesting the act. Some of these resolutions even instruct city employees and local law enforcement not to assist in investigations they believe violate individuals' constitutional rights to privacy and freedom. Disparate groups such as the National Rifle Association and the American Civil Liberties Union that are typically at odds with each other about legislation have joined forces to voice their mutual concerns over the USA Patriot Act and its proposed sequel, the Domestic Security Enhancement Act (often called Patriot Act II).

Patriot Act Critics and Proponents

Critics of the Patriot Act argue that authorities already had the necessary tools at their disposal to monitor suspected terrorists. "The civil liberties of ordinary Americans have taken a tremendous blow with this law," wrote the editors of the Electronic Frontier Foundation (EFF). "Yet there is no evidence that our previous civil liberties posed a barrier to the effective tracking or prosecution of terrorists. In fact, the government made no showing that the previous powers of law enforcement and intelligence agencies to spy on US citizens were insufficient to allow them to investigate and prosecute acts of terrorism."[38]

Proponents of the legislation, however, argue that the time involved in obtaining court approval for search warrants, subpoenas, and wiretaps hindered organizations such as the FBI from acting swiftly when dealing with terrorists. They justify sweeping legal changes by saying that U.S. law must keep up with technological advances if the U.S. government is to maintain the advantage over terrorist groups. In defense of the Patriot Act, President Bush told reporters, "We're dealing with terrorists who operate by highly sophisticated methods and technologies, some of which were not even available when our existing laws were written."[39]

This tension between civil rights and national security measures is nothing new. It is a debate that is as old as the United States itself. However, U.S. intelligence agencies

Attorney General John Ashcroft asks the House Judiciary Committee to approve measures that would expand the powers of law enforcement under the Patriot Act.

are now asked to identify suspects who live among the citizens of this country and may even be citizens. They must search through all the countries of the world to find a small number of al-Qaeda members—and Osama bin Laden in particular. And they have been asked to identify potential terrorists who may be plotting violent acts at home or abroad. In order to identify suspects and prevent attacks, the U.S. intelligence community has devised a number of useful techniques—some of them old and some new, many of them controversial—to use in the fight against terrorism.

Chapter Four

Following the Money Trail

As the hunt for the mastermind behind the September 11 attacks began, the prime suspect was Osama bin Laden and his terrorist network, al-Qaeda. Although bin Laden had previously made veiled threats that his organization would be launching a terrorist attack on Americans, al-Qaeda did not explicitly claim responsibility for the events of September 11. U.S. government officials, however, including President George W. Bush, were certain that al-Qaeda was behind the attacks and wanted to use the U.S. military to destroy the organization. However, in order to do so, they had to invade Afghanistan, the country harboring bin Laden and other al-Qaeda leaders. In order to secure international support for this invasion, the Bush administration needed to provide world leaders who were skeptical about al-Qaeda's involvement with evidence linking bin Laden and his organization to the hijackers. President Bush asked the intelligence community to provide this evidence.

Investigators reasoned that the best way to prove that bin Laden was behind the attacks was to show that he had paid for them. In order to do this, they needed to trace the hijackers' purchases all the way back to their source, which the investigators suspected would be bin Laden's fortune. The terrorists who had flown planes into the World Trade Center would thus be definitively linked to bin Laden. The U.S. intelligence officials also saw following the money trail as a way to deter future attacks, since discovering how al-Qaeda made and moved money would allow them to freeze and seize its assets. This in turn would cut off al-Qaeda's funding and limit the resources at its disposal to plan future attacks.

Finding the Bank Accounts of Terrorists

One week after the September 11 attacks, investigators set out on the money trail, hoping it would allow them to link the bank accounts of the hijackers to Osama bin Laden. They began with what they knew—the names of the nineteen men who had seized control of four planes and flown three of them into targets. On September 18, the U.S. Federal Reserve ordered all banks, domestic and foreign, under its jurisdiction to search through their records for any accounts or transactions involving the nineteen people identified by the FBI as the hijackers.

Once investigators located an account, they then had the ability to track the withdrawals and deposits made. Thus investigators were reportedly able to link hijacker Mohammed

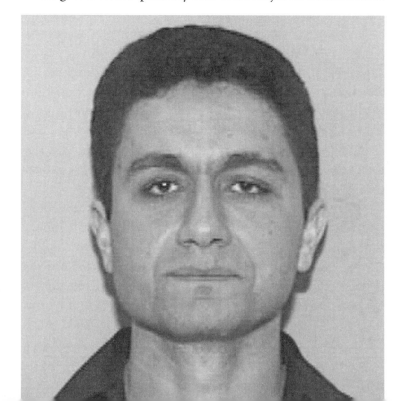

Hijacker-terrorist Mohammed Atta participated in money-laundering networks to finance the September 11 attacks.

Atta with more than one hundred thousand dollars that was wired to him from Egypt, the United Arab Emirates, and Pakistan. Atta distributed the funds to the other hijackers by sending them multiple money orders for small sums. Intelligence reports indicate that just before the attacks, Atta and two other hijackers sent roughly twenty thousand dollars back to Dubai to the account of Mustapha Ahmed al-Hawsawi, thought to be the man who set up bin Laden's fund-raising and money-laundering networks in the 1990s.

While discoveries such as this do not directly link hijackers to bin Laden, they do point to a connection. In the weeks and months after September 11, the Central Intelligence Agency (CIA) and the Federal Bureau of Investigation (FBI) discovered a number of connections of this sort. This financial trail combined with other evidence led many world leaders to conclude that bin Laden was indeed behind the attacks, and on those grounds they offered assistance to the United States.

Making Money

The CIA and FBI did not follow the money trail just to link the hijackers with bin Laden; they also hoped to learn how al-Qaeda made and laundered money so that they could prevent further access to these funds. In late October 2001, the U.S. government announced Operation Green Quest, an interagency task force with top investigators from the FBI and the CIA as well as the Treasury Department and the U.S. Customs Service. According to Deputy Treasury Secretary Kenneth Dam, the operation was designed to "deny terrorist groups access to [banks around the world] . . . impair the ability of terrorists to fundraise, and to expose [and seize terrorist funds]."[40]

The task force discovered that al-Qaeda had set up a number of legitimate businesses whose profits went to fund the organization. These were businesses with bona fide employees working and earning wages. The businesses actually

An Islamic woman from Michigan speaks at a press conference after her husband was deported. He was arrested on suspicion of raising money for terrorist organizations.

produced a product or service, and each year the business's profits went to al-Qaeda. Al-Qaeda's legitimate business holdings included corporations set up by bin Laden, a network of Middle Eastern honey traders, and gem miners in Tanzania. While all these businesses deny ties to bin Laden, CIA officers who spoke to local miners found a more salient connection. "Yes, people here are [working] for Osama," Musa Abdallah, a Kenyan who has worked as a tanzanite miner for six years, told the *Wall Street Journal*. "Just look around and you will find serious Muslims who believe in him and work for him."[41]

In addition to legitimate businesses, al-Qaeda also engages in a number of criminal enterprises to make money. Theft, fraud, and smuggling are just some of the crimes al-Qaeda cells are encouraged to participate in to support themselves. Credit card fraud—the theft of credit card numbers followed by either the illegal use of them and/or the selling of the numbers—has proven to be a valuable endeavor for a variety of terrorist organizations. Al-Qaeda members may also smuggle contraband items from one country to another. Apparently, the border region where Argentina, Brazil, and Paraguay meet is one area where Muslim traders thought to be supporting al-Qaeda work as smugglers to make money for the organization. These activities are difficult for U.S. intelligence agencies to track down and stop since transactions are carried out using mostly cash or goods, which cannot be tracked as easily as a legitimate business's bank records.

Pakistani president General Pervez Musharraf (left) praises the efforts of U.S. treasury secretary Paul O'Neill (right) to stop the flow of money to terrorist groups.

Support Your Local al-Qaeda?

Legitimate businesses and criminal enterprises give al-Qaeda some money with which to work, but the bulk of the organization's wealth comes from fund-raising and donations. While some of these funds are obtained legitimately from donors who wish to support the organization, some are obtained illegally by tricking people into believing their money is going to support humanitarian, charitable causes.

There are a large number of Islamic charities around the world, the majority of which are completely legitimate. The prevalence of charities within the Islamic community is tied to one of the fundamental doctrines of Islam, *zakat* or alms-giving. According to the Koran, the holy book of Islam, just as all Muslims have an obligation to worship, so too do they share in an obligation to the social welfare of their community. It is therefore the religious duty of all Muslims to donate 2.5 percent of their annual income to help the poor and needy. The Koran specifies eight different types of "poor and needy" people who can receive *zakat*, one of which is those "in service of the cause of God." Therefore, some Muslims who believe that al-Qaeda is defending the Islamic faith and Muslim people give their yearly *zakat* to the organization.

However, other al-Qaeda financial supporters may never know that their funds are going to the organization. Al-Qaeda uses some seemingly humanitarian charities as fronts to siphon off funds. In this way, some legitimate charities, mosques, websites, and wealthy individuals are duped into supporting al-Qaeda unwittingly. It is a win-win situation for al-Qaeda. The false charities provide knowing donors with cover should their donations be tracked, while simultaneously bringing in funds from unwitting donors. The case of Saudi Arabia's Princess Haifa clearly illustrates this point. The princess is the wife of Prince Bandar, the Saudi ambassador to the United States. In December 2002, U.S. intelligence authorities discovered that a check written by the princess was used to finance two of the September 11 hijack-

ers. The princess originally wrote the check to a woman who claimed it would go to help her ailing family member. However, the check never financed this charitable cause. Instead, the woman signed it over to a man who made a loan to the hijackers. While some speculate that the princess knew where the money would end up, others classify the incident as a charitable donation gone astray.

The U.S. intelligence community has been able to take action against some of al-Qaeda's charitable money sources. For instance, when FBI and CIA agents scrutinized the known bank accounts belonging to al-Qaeda, on numerous occasions they found that the same account number was being used by a (supposed) humanitarian relief organization. Once the scam was discovered, a number of U.S.-based Islamic charities, including the Holy Land Foundation for Relief and Development, were shut down. Intelligence agencies also discovered charitable organizations with ties to al-Qaeda in

FBI agents and New York police detectives load evidence taken from a Hatikva Identity Jewish center in Brooklyn. The center is suspected of raising money for al-Qaeda.

Pakistan, Kuwait, and Saudi Arabia, and asked the governments of these nations to shut down the charities.

A great deal of al-Qaeda's financial support comes from solicitations of wealthy donors, and so the CIA directly targeted individuals who gave money to the terrorist group. Many of these wealthy supporters reside in the Middle East, in places like Egypt and Saudi Arabia. The Saudi Arabian government was reluctant to help U.S. officials track down its influential citizens and refused to grant the CIA unfettered access to suspicious bank accounts. "Frustrated, the CIA took matters into its own hands," writes reporter David Kaplan, "hacking into Middle Eastern bank accounts to chart the flow of funds to al Qaeda operatives. . . . Other times, case officers offered bribes and came away with bank statements and account numbers."[42]

The CIA also targeted al-Qaeda's solicitors (individuals who ask for money on behalf of an organization) by setting

Yemeni women demand the release of Mohammed Ali Hasan al-Moayad from a German prison. Al-Moayad reportedly raised funds for al-Qaeda and Hamas.

up sting operations to ensnare them. For example, in March 2003 the CIA targeted a cleric from Yemen named Sheik Mohammed Ali Hasan al-Moayad, who it believed was instrumental in soliciting donations to support Islamic terrorist organizations. The sting operation occurred in Frankfurt, Germany, where German and American intelligence officials used an informant al-Moayad knew in order to lure him to a bugged hotel room. Al-Moayad held a number of meetings in this room with intelligence officers listening to every word. Once they had gleaned all the information al-Moayad knew from listening in on his conversations, the intelligence officers set a trap. They had a second informant pose as a wealthy American Muslim wanting to donate to al-Qaeda. He told al-Moayad he wanted to donate $2 million for jihad, to be split between al-Qaeda and Hamas (a Palestinian terrorist organization). When al-Moayad took the bait, he was arrested.

The efforts of the CIA analysts quite literally paid dividends. Through the tracking of terrorist funds by the U.S. intelligence community, U.S. authorities were able to seize well over $100 million in the first year. In fact, their methods were so effective that by June 2003, reporter David Kaplan was able to write that al-Qaeda's "once bountiful finances ... have become precarious. One recent intercept revealed a terrorist pleading for $80."[43]

Laundering Money

Even after the U.S. intelligence community damaged some of al-Qaeda's financial resources by targeting wealthy solicitors and donors and closing down al-Qaeda charities, businesses, and criminal enterprises, the financially robust organization still managed to make a great deal of money. Much of this money was not detected by U.S. intelligence authorities because it was expertly laundered. After September 11, the FBI and CIA set out to better understand the methods used by al-Qaeda to launder money so that they could deprive the organization of these funds as well.

Yemeni police stand guard outside the German embassy in Yemen, where a large group of protestors gathered in defense of al-Moayad.

Laundering money employs a variety of techniques to conceal the illegal origins of funds so they can be used to purchase goods and services. For example, if a man showed up at an American bank asking to open an account and deposit $100,000 in cash that he claimed he had found, the bank would alert the FBI and CIA immediately because it would be fairly obvious the money was dirty, or obtained through illegal means. However, the man would arouse much less suspicion if he bought fifteen "shell" corporations, fake companies that exist only on paper. Shell companies are sold on the black market and typically cost less than $1,000. Each fake company usually comes with a mailing address, a fax number, and the name of a nonexistent company owner. The man could then set up fifteen separate bank accounts in different locations and deposit differing sums from $2,000 to $9,999 (he would want to stay under $10,000 since most banks have to report any transaction over that amount). If the man went to these lengths, the fact that the money was originally illegal would most likely go unnoticed by the authorities.

Moving money is another important part of money laundering. The idea is to transfer funds to different locations and convert them into many different currencies so that they can no longer be traced back to their source. It is difficult to move large sums of money through traditional banking institutions without attracting attention, which is good for the intelligence agencies. However, terrorists have found several ways to get around this difficulty.

Al-Qaeda is known to use its worldwide network of charities and legitimate businesses to move money through over-invoicing. In this type of money laundering, a business that

U.S. Customs agents seize evidence of an al-Qaeda money-laundering operation in Massachusetts.

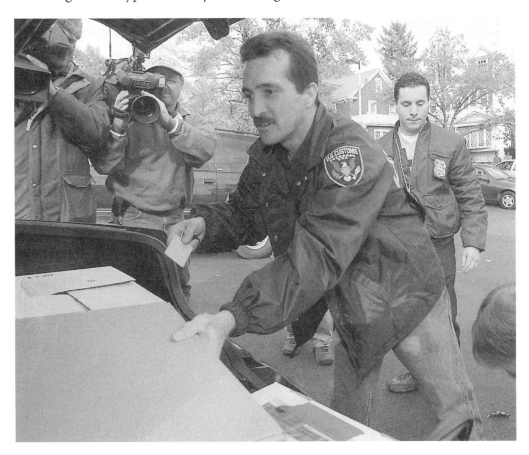

actually exists and provides a good or service is used. Money launderers then justify the movement of large sums of money by creating invoices either for amounts that far exceed the worth of the goods or for goods that never existed. For example, if a wealthy American wanted to give al-Qaeda $200,000, he could donate that amount to a local charity that was really a front for al-Qaeda. If al-Qaeda wanted these funds to support an operation in Pakistan, it might arrange for the charity to do business with an al-Qaeda–directed outfit there—for instance, a fabric manufacturer in Karachi. The charity would order fabric worth $2,000; the manufacturer would deliver the fabric to the United States, but charge the charity an extra $200,000 for it, for a total invoice of $202,000 for the fabric. The invoice would make the payment look legitimate and could be shown to both the American and Pakistani authorities. Therefore, the money could be deposited into the fabric company's bank account in Karachi, where it would be available for redirection to al-Qaeda cells in Pakistan.

Another method used to move money is called smurfing. This process breaks money that needs to be transferred into smaller amounts so that its movement will not be noticed by authorities. Smurfing exploits the fact that banks do not have to report transactions under a certain dollar amount to international banking authorities, usually $10,000. Once the money is broken into small amounts, the smurfing begins. For instance, an al-Qaeda member who had to send $50,000 to the organization's leadership would write many checks for small amounts from a variety of different banks, making certain not to repeat transactions too frequently. Then, al-Qaeda would hope that these small sums got lost among the millions of movements of money every day.

Hawala

One thing that makes al-Qaeda and other terrorist funds quite difficult for the U.S. intelligence community to track is the terrorists' use of the *hawala* system to move money.

Hawala—also called *hundi* and *chop*—is an ancient informal banking system prevalent in the Middle East, Asia, and Southeast Asia. *Hawala* is a legitimate way of moving money that is used by numerous law-abiding citizens each year. However, *hawala* transfers money without actually moving it, leaves no paper trail, reaches the farthest corners of the globe, is unregulated, and provides anonymous services. This makes it an ideal way for terrorists to transfer funds as well.

Hawala is a complex system that relies largely on trust. It depends on brokers called *hawaladars* who operate all over the world. To understand how *hawala* works, imagine that a person in one city needs to send money to someone in another. The sender contacts her local *hawaladar* and gives him the money (in her country's currency) she wishes to send. The *hawaladar* accepts the money along with a fee for his work. He in turn gives the sender a code, which she passes on to the person who will receive the money. In the meantime, the *hawaladar* contacts a fellow broker who has a *hawala* operation in the recipient's city. This broker agrees to distribute money from his own resources to the recipient. The recipient contacts this same *hawaladar* and gives him the code. This proves she is the money's intended recipient, and she receives (in her own country's currency) the amount of money deposited by the original sender. Once the transaction is complete, all records are destroyed.

There is no paper trail of the transaction remaining, no wire transfers, no government regulation, not even a bank. No money actually moves. *Hawaladars* keep track of how much money they owe each other and either this amount evens out in subsequent transactions or they settle their debts at a later date in gold. While *hawala* provides a number of social benefits by allowing people to quickly and easily send money to their family members in remote locations across the world, it is also very useful for terrorist organizations that wish to move money without its being noticed or tracked.

For example, al-Qaeda cells in India can give their local *hawaladar* a large sum of money in Indian rupees and ask

U.S. Customs agents seize evidence of a major operation. Stringent anti-money-laundering legislation has made it easier for authorities to crack down on such operations.

that these funds be converted into Canadian dollars and supplied to a sleeper cell in Canada. The entire exchange can be done in the time it takes to make a phone call. Once the transaction is complete, the recipients will have cash in Canadian dollars and the records of the transaction will be destroyed. Thus, investigators can never seize records that link the two terrorist cells. The large sum of money has been moved across the globe without the physical sending of actual money to tip off authorities or the generation of any records.

The CIA and FBI have little chance of tracking or stopping the transfer of terrorist funds through the *hawala* system. However, they were able to crack down on some al-Qaeda money-laundering activities through the passage of stringent anti-money-laundering legislation in the United

States and by rallying international cooperation to help them seize terrorist funds in banks around the world. In so doing, they were able to show that the September 11 hijackers were funded by al-Qaeda and to assemble support from nations around the world to invade Afghanistan to destroy the organization and its leader, Osama bin Laden. These actions had a decided effect on al-Qaeda's financial resources and thus its ability to mount further attacks on American targets.

Chapter Five

Sounding the Alarm

Among the many losses of September 11 was Americans' sense of insulation and security. People wondered if it was too risky to work in skyscrapers or whether a trip to the mall or a sporting event might end in disaster. Many U.S. citizens desired access to accurate information about the level of danger in the country and specific steps they could take to remain safe. However, the government had no defined system to distribute such information to the populace.

Therefore, in the months after the September 11 attacks, U.S. officials worked to establish an effective system to disperse accurate information to the public about the probability of terrorist attacks. The distribution of this information benefited not only American civilians, but also the U.S. intelligence community and others trying to deter terrorist attack. Since accurate information about the level of danger in the country might minimize the number of people at vulnerable targets, sounding the alarm seemed like a logical way to prevent mass casualties in an attack—and possibly the attack itself.

The FBI's Early Warnings

It took a good deal of trial and error to create an effective system to disperse information. Immediately after the attacks, it seemed as though almost every governmental entity had cause to warn the people living in the United States. Hungry media often spread this information in an alarming manner, and people became very confused about the degree of danger they faced when riding the bus in the morning or flying to see relatives.

Initially, the FBI was in charge of counseling the public about possible terrorist attacks. The FBI issued four warnings in five months—two in October 2001, one covering the one-month anniversary of September 11 and another toward month's end; one in December 2001, in part because of the convergence of Ramadan, Hanukkah, Christmas, and New Year's Eve (intelligence officials believed this convergence of holidays might be an attractive target time for al-Qaeda); another in January 2002 for the Olympic games; and another in February 2002 when the FBI "identified a man from

National Guardsmen patrol San Francisco's Golden Gate Bridge after the government issued a warning that terrorists might target major bridges in California.

Yemen or Saudi Arabia as planning an attack on U.S. interests in the homeland or abroad."[44]

The warning announced by Attorney General John Ashcroft on October 29, 2001, was indicative of the vague sort of information that Americans were given about the threat of attack. Ashcroft told reporters that "intelligence sources had found 'credible' information the nation could be the focus for some sort of terrorist attack within the week . . . [and] called on law enforcement agencies, citizens and U.S. interests abroad to be on 'highest alert.'"[45] When reporters pressed further, all Ashcroft or FBI director Robert S. Mueller would say was that the information was credible, but they had no idea when the attack might occur or what the target might be. They told people to be vigilant and take precautions, but also to go about their lives.

FBI director Mueller (left) explains the rationale behind the terrorist warning issued on October 29, 2001, as Attorney General Ashcroft (right) looks on.

The warning on December 3, 2001, was similarly ambiguous: "The information we have does not point to any specific target either in America or abroad, and it does not outline any specific type of attack," Homeland Security director Tom Ridge announced. "However, the analysts who review this information believe the quantity and level of threats are above the norm and have reached a threshold where we should once again place the public on general alert."[46]

Angry critics charged that the FBI's warnings were too vague and that no one knew what to do in response to them—people were told only that something could go horribly wrong at some time in some place. In addition, the FBI warning system was said to lack the complexity that would allow the American public to know the severity and nature of the terrorist threat. People had no idea how likely an attack was to occur or whether that attack would be catastrophic or on a smaller scale. Because of these shortcomings, some critics speculated that the only thing FBI warnings were good for was feeding public anxieties about terrorist attacks and instilling fear in the general populace.

The Homeland Security Advisory System

In response to these critics and in an effort to cull information from a variety of sources and disseminate it to people living in and visiting the United States, the Bush administration created the Department of Homeland Security (DHS) in January 2002. The DHS coordinated twenty-two agencies that had previously worked independently into one department in an effort to provide better communication between the agencies and protect the nation against terrorism. Later, the administration initiated the Homeland Security Advisory System to alert the American public about domestic terrorist threats.

The presidential directive that established the Homeland Security Advisory System said, "The Nation requires a Homeland Security Advisory System to provide a comprehensive and effective means to disseminate information

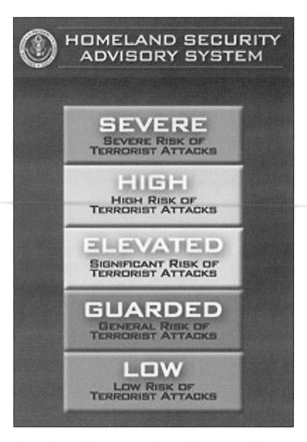

HOMELAND SECURITY
ADVISORY SYSTEM

SEVERE
SEVERE RISK OF
TERRORIST ATTACKS

HIGH
HIGH RISK OF
TERRORIST ATTACKS

ELEVATED
SIGNIFICANT RISK OF
TERRORIST ATTACKS

GUARDED
GENERAL RISK OF
TERRORIST ATTACKS

LOW
LOW RISK OF
TERRORIST ATTACKS

The color-coded Homeland Security Advisory System keeps Americans aware of the likelihood of terrorist attack.

regarding the risk of terrorist acts."[47] It further stated that the system was intended to create a common vocabulary for a discussion about threats as well as provide appropriate actions for citizens to take in response. The new system took the authority to issue threat warnings away from the FBI and gave it instead to the attorney general, who was urged to consult with the Homeland Security office.

The advisory system ranks the danger posed by terrorist threats in five levels, or conditions, each with its own color. The lowest threat level, green, is appropriately labeled Low. This is followed by the blue level, Guarded; yellow, Elevated; orange, High; and red, Severe. Each warning level has corresponding "protective measures" that citizens and businesses are encouraged to take in order to ensure their safety. This facet of the system helps to deter attack since businesses, government offices, airports, and public venues all increase security measures in accordance with the threat level, thus making it more difficult for a terrorist cell to infiltrate and attack. As *New York Times* reporter Eric Lichtblau explains, "There are . . . any number of border security measures [that are increased] in response to [an elevated threat level]: Tightening airport security, putting more air marshals in the sky; doing additional photo I.D. checks, inspections. There is a long list of steps that . . . will be immediately implemented because of [an] elevated status."[48]

The CIA's role in this advisory system was clear from the moment it was conceived. The presidential directive that established the advisory system stated that the agency was charged with providing "a continuous and timely flow of inte-grated threat assessments and reports"[49] to those who deter-mine the threat level. In other words, it was the CIA's job to gather intelligence that would help determine the nation's threat level.

The Difficulties of Determining the Threat Level

Determining the threat level, and consequently how con-cerned the average citizen should be and the precautions that should be taken, is the most complicated part of the Homeland Security Advisory System. Intelligence analysts have to consider a number of factors. They must examine the quantity and quality of information gathered from sources, evaluate the credibility of those sources, determine whether they corroborate or contradict each other, decide whether

President George Bush (right) welcomes Tom Ridge (left) to his new position as secretary director of the Department of Homeland Security.

threats are vague or specific, and consider what important world events, anniversaries, and religious events might trigger terrorist action.

When the sheer number of factors is taken into consideration, it becomes apparent that assessing the threat level is part science and part art. It is also an enormous task. The CIA intercepts more communications in one day than it can process in a week, and the FBI receives tips on thousands of threats each day. The vast majority of these are of little interest to terrorist investigations. Routine cell phone calls between law-abiding citizens and bluffs made by kooks or pranksters are not of interest to national defense. A truly menacing threat can easily get lost in the midst of all this excess information.

Of course, it is extremely unlikely that U.S. intelligence agencies will intercept a call in which a man identifies himself as an al-Qaeda operative and discloses the organization's plans for the next act of catastrophic terrorism. In fact, the U.S. intelligence community has found it nearly impossible to infiltrate al-Qaeda through espionage and gain access to this sort of information. The resulting irony is that not only do the CIA and FBI have too much useless information to wade through, but they also lack access to important information about huge threats. They must therefore try to piece together small bits of information in order to detect threats.

Intelligence Chatter and Nonspecific Threats

The intelligence community begins to assess a threat by paying close attention to any cultural, political, or religious events that may mobilize terrorists to strike. *New York Times* reporter Eric Lichtblau explains that "one thing that the analysts and the F.B.I. and the C.I.A. look for is a trigger point. . . . Is there something on the calendar or anniversary of some date that is likely to prompt some sort of symbolic attack?"[50] For example, threat levels were raised on September 11, 2002, because officials were worried that the anniversary of the attacks might inspire terrorists to strike again.

Even when they cannot decode messages, CIA and FBI analysts can monitor the frequency of communication between terrorists—that is, how often they speak to each other—in order to determine the threat level. This type of monitoring is called traffic analysis. In much the same way that newscasters look at car traffic on U.S. roads to predict the time it will take drivers to complete their commute, FBI and CIA analysts look at communications traffic (how much of it there is, where it is going, and how often certain groups of people are communicating) to predict whether or not there is something to be concerned

As Homeland Security secretary, Tom Ridge hopes the department will be able to analyze intelligence information with greater efficiency than the FBI and CIA.

about. They cannot get access to the content of many of these communications, but they can notice increased traffic, called surges in communication. These surges frequently precede an attempted terrorist attack. "There was a surge about the time [shoe-bomber] Richard Reid got on the plane," says one analyst. "We would get surges, and then you would hear about [terrorists] who were stopped."[51]

The information that CIA and FBI analysts monitor with traffic analysis is frequently referred to as intelligence chatter. Intelligence chatter is a collection of all the information—seemingly important or not—that comes into the CIA about a group, event, or other topic. It can be monitored both for volume and content. In much the same way that individual geese

George Tenet, director of the CIA, was criticized for the agency's failure to prevent the September 11, 2001, terrorist attacks.

in a flock begin to chatter right before the flock takes flight, terrorist organizations begin to chatter right before they launch attacks. For instance, prior to September 11, the intelligence chatter increased drastically in volume. This spike in chatter led analysts to believe that a plan was being put in motion. However, they were unable to determine what that plan was.

Similar spikes in intelligence chatter have been seen since the attacks and often play a critical role in determining the threat level. Increases in chatter combined with information from credible sources cause the threat level to be raised, whereas a reduction in chatter can cause it to be lowered. In April 2003, the threat level was lowered from orange to yellow due to what reporters Jeanne Meserve and Mike Ahlers explain was a "decrease in the volume of intelligence chatter, and the intelligence that was continuing to come in was from a narrower range of sources, and from sources not considered highly credible."[52] However, the level was raised to orange again in late May 2003 based on an increase in intelligence chatter.

While intelligence analysts who monitor chatter may suspect that an attack is in the works, they frequently cannot offer any specific information about the pending attack, either because they simply do not know the details or because revealing the information would further endanger security. In fact, alerts based on levels of intelligence chatter are by their very nature vague, or what analysts call nonspecific. In some cases, the CIA and FBI may even have a lead on what type of targets the terrorists are going after—for instance, in a February 2003 threat level increase, authorities warned that al-Qaeda was going after targets such as apartment buildings or targets within the Jewish community. However, nonspecific threats are, as their name suggests, nonspecific, and intelligence agencies often have no idea against whom the attack is planned, where it will occur, what type of attack it will be, or when it will happen.

Critics of the System

While some citizens feel protected and informed as a result of the changing threat levels, critics of the advisory system complain that the warnings are too vague to be effective and therefore serve only to make citizens anxious and fearful. "Ridge's warning lights are meant to reflect the terrorist threat, but instead they are cause for confusion and a staple joke on late-night television," writer John Miller says. "People don't need a set of lights with vague significance; they need useful information and practical advice."[53]

Some critics suggest that the system exists only to absolve the government from any blame for not warning citizens. "The only thing warnings this vague are good for is providing political cover in case of disaster," a *New York Times* editorial contends. "They offer no specific information about the location, timing or method of attack, and are all but useless to the average citizen, or even to local law enforcement officers."[54] The *Times* opinion seems to be shared by many Americans. According to a poll conducted by the Answer Institute for Homeland Security, more than two-thirds of Americans found the Homeland Security Advisory System an ineffective way of informing the public about terrorist threats.

In addition to criticisms that the information conveyed by the system is useless, some people complain that raising and lowering the threat level costs states a great deal of money. In public venues and businesses around the nation, additional security guards must be hired, bridges must be closed, city and state budgets must be increased to keep more police officers and firefighters on duty. In fact, after the level was raised from yellow to orange and back again in May/June of 2003, the state of Arizona began to consider not following the advice of the advisory system. "It creates incredible problems: overtime, financial, functional," said Frank Navarrete, the state's homeland security director. "It's not quite to the point where it creates havoc, but it's quite disruptive."[55] This poses an entirely new problem for advocates of a national warning system since it is difficult for it to be effective if each state begins to interpret the threat level in its own way.

When the national terror alert is raised, additional security personnel are called to duty. Here, a member of the Coast Guard scans the Detroit River during a heightened terror alert.

This woman lost her job because she refused to fly to a business meeting during a heightened terror alert. Airlines are struggling as a result of the Homeland Security Advisory System.

Whether or not the Homeland Security Advisory System remains in place, the terrorist threat will persist, and the task of assessing this threat will fall to the intelligence community. Determining the threat level is both a science and an art, and it is hoped that as the CIA and FBI practice this art form, they will eventually perfect how to use it.

Notes

Introduction: "We Didn't Know What We Knew"

1. Quoted in Judith Miller, Jeff Gerth, and Don Van Natta Jr., "Missed Signals: Many Say U.S. Planned for Terror but Failed to Take Action," *New York Times*, December 30, 2001. www.nytimes.com.

2. CNN, "Agent: 'Moussaoui could fly . . . into the WTC,'" May 14, 2002. www.cnn.com.

3. David Brooks, "The Elephantiasis of Reason," *Atlantic Monthly*, January/February 2003. www.theatlantic.com.

Chapter One: A Unique Enemy

4. Quoted in Stephen Cass, "Listening In: Are the Glory Days of Electronic Spying over—or Just Beginning?" *IEEE Spectrum*, April 2003, p. 35.

5. Carl Conetta, "Dislocating Alcyoneus: How to Combat al-Qaeda and the New Terrorism" (Project on Defense Alternatives Briefing Memo #23), June 25, 2002. www.comw.org/pda.

6. Quoted in Belinda Rhodes, "Al-Qaeda's Continuing Threat," March 11, 2002. http://news.bbc.co.uk.

7. Maurice Greenberg et al., *Terrorist Financing: Report of an Independent Task Force Sponsored by the Council of Foreign Relations*. New York: Council of Foreign Relations, 2002, p. 5.

8. Greenberg et al., *Terrorist Financing*, p. 5.

9. Chitra Ragavan, "Mueller's Mandate: The FBI Chief Has a Little Job to Do—Overhaul the Agency from Top to Bottom," *U.S. News & World Report*, May 26, 2003. www.usnews.com.

10. Quoted in Brian Ross, "Hunting Bin Laden: Delta Force Has Been Practicing in Afghanistan Since 1998, Says Author," September 27, 2001. www.ABCNews.com.

11. Stephen Budiansky, "Losing the Code War: The Great Age of Code Breaking Is over—and with It Much of Our Ability to

Track the Communications of Our Enemies," *Atlantic Monthly*, February 2002. www.theatlantic.com.

12. Al-Qaeda Training Manual. www.usdoj.com.

13. Quoted in Ross, "Hunting Bin Laden."

14. Reuel Marc Gerecht, "The Counterterrorist Myth: A Former CIA Operative Explains Why the Terrorist Usama bin Ladin Has Little to Fear from American Intelligence," *Atlantic Monthly*, July/August 2001. www.theatlantic.com.

15. Quoted in Gerecht, "The Counterterrorist Myth."

16. Osama bin Laden, *Jihad* Against the Jews and Crusaders: World Islamic Front Statement," February 23, 1998. www.fas.org.

17. Quoted in Paul J. Smith, "Transnational Terrorism and the al Qaeda Model: Confronting New Realities," *Parameters*, Summer 2002, p. 39.

18. CNN, "Target Terrorism: The Investigation Continues; Intelligence Community Retraces Its Steps; How Can Attacks Be Prevented?" aired October 6, 2001. Excerpted transcript available at www.cia.gov.

Chapter Two: Using Technology to Thwart Terrorism

19. David J. Rothkopf, "Business Versus Terrorism," *Foreign Policy*, May/June 2002. www.foreignpolicy.com.

20. Budiansky, "Losing the Code War."

21. Ragavan, "Mueller's Mandate."

22. Ragavan, "Mueller's Mandate."

23. Elsa M. Wenzel, "FBI Computers Enter the 21st Century," *PC World*, April 3, 2003. www.pcworld.com.

24. Defense Advanced Research Projects Agency's Website. www.darpa.mil.

25. Quoted in *Wired*, "Total Info System Totally Touchy," December 2, 2002. www.wired.com.

26. Quoted in *Wired*, "Total Info System Totally Touchy."

27. Colin Soloway, Rod Nordland, and Barbie Nadeau, "Hiding (and

Seeking) Messages on the Web," *Newsweek*, June 17, 2002. www.freelists.org.

28. Timothy Thomas, "Al Qaeda and the Internet: The Danger of 'Cyberplanning,'" *Parameters*, Spring 2003, p. 112.

29. Soloway, Nordland, and Nadeau, "Hiding (and Seeking) Messages on the Web."

30. Quoted in Soloway, Nordland, and Nadeau, "Hiding (and Seeking) Messages on the Web."

Chapter Three: Identifying Suspects and Tightening Security

31. Charles C. Mann, "Homeland Insecurity: A Top Expert Says America's Approach to Protecting Itself Will Only Make Matters Worse, Forget 'Foolproof' Technology—We Need Systems Designed to Fail Smartly," *Atlantic Monthly*, September 2002. www.theatlantic.com.

32. BBC News, "Hi-Tech Security Flaws Exposed," May 31, 2002. http://news.bbc.co.uk.

33. David Kaplan, "Playing Offense: The Inside Story of How U.S. Terrorist Hunters Are Going After al Qaeda," *U.S. News & World Report*, June 2, 2003. www.usnews.com.

34. Quoted in Ragavan, "Mueller's Mandate."

35. Quoted in *NewsHour with Jim Lehrer*, "Liberty vs. Security," September 10, 2002. www.pbs.org.

36. Quoted in Ragavan, "Mueller's Mandate."

37. Quoted in Ragavan, "Mueller's Mandate."

38. Electronic Frontier Foundation, "EFF Analysis of the Provisions of the USA PATRIOT Act That Relate to Online Activities," October 31, 2001. www.eff.org.

39. Quoted in *NewsHour with Jim Lehrer*, "The Patriot Act," February 12, 2003. www.pbs.org.

Chapter Four: Following the Money Trail

40. *NewsMax.com Wires*, "Govt. Launches Operation to Deny Terrorists Financing," October 26, 2001. www.NewsMax.com.

41. Robert Block and Daniel Pearl, "Underground Trade: Much-Smuggled Gem Called Tanzanite Helps Bin Laden Supporters," *Wall Street Journal*, November 16, 2001.

42. Kaplan, "Playing Offense."

43. Kaplan, "Playing Offense."

Chapter Five: Sounding The Alarm

44. Rey Ko Huang, "Terror Alerts: The Homeland Security Advisory System," April 22, 2002. www.cdi.org.

45. CNN, "Ashcroft: New Terror Attack Possible," October 29, 2001. www.cnn.com.

46. ABCNews.com, "New Threats: U.S. Urged to Remain on High Alert," December 3, 2001. www.ABCNews.com.

47. Office of the Press Secretary, "Homeland Security Presidential Directive-3." www.whitehouse.gov.

48. Quoted in *NewsHour with Jim Lehrer*, "Terror Alert," February 7, 2003. www.pbs.org.

49. Office of the Press Secretary, "Homeland Security Presidential Directive-3."

50. Quoted in *NewsHour with Jim Lehrer*, "Terror Alert."

51. Quoted in Soloway, Nordland, and Nadeau, "Hiding (and Seeking) Messages on the Web."

52. Jeanne Meserve and Mike Ahlers, "Terror Threat Lowered to Yellow," April 16, 2003. www.cnn.com.

53. Quoted in Greg Barber, "Homeland Security Advisory System." www.pbs.org.

54. Quoted in Barber, "Homeland Security Advisory System."

55. Quoted in Judy Nichols, "Arizona May Ignore Next Orange Alert," *Arizona Republic*, June 1, 2003. www.azcentral.com.

For Further Reading

Internet Sources

BBCNews, "Hi-Tech Security Flaws Exposed," May 31, 2002. http://news.bbc.co.uk. The article contains an interesting discussion about how experts have tricked a number of the new, high-tech security devices.

David Kaplan, "Playing Offense: The Inside Story of How U.S. Terrorist Hunters Are Going After al Qaeda," *U.S. News & World Report*, June 2, 2003. www.usnews.com. An excellent account of the many ways that the CIA and FBI have been tracking down and capturing terrorists since September 11.

Chitra Ragavan, "Mueller's Mandate: The FBI Chief Has a Little Job to Do—Overhaul the Agency from Top to Bottom," *U.S. News & World Report*, May 26, 2003. www.usnews.com. A detailed explanation of the problems faced by the FBI post–September 11 and the solutions being implemented.

Websites

The CIA's Website for Kids (www.odci.gov) Descriptions of the CIA, how it operates, and what different staff members do. Also, some fun games and links to other government organizations' websites.

The FBI's Website for Kids Grades 6 Through 12 (www. fbi. gov/kids/htm). Descriptions of the FBI, investigations, games, a discussion about working dogs, and adventures.

The *New York Times* Learning Network (www.nytimes.com/learning). Designed for grades three–twelve, a number of useful and well written articles can be found about September 11, the CIA, and the FBI.

***Time* for Kids Online** (www.timeforkids.com/TFK). *Time* magazine's kids' version. Contains a number of well-written articles about September 11 as well as games and research tools.

Works Consulted

Publications

Maurice Greenberg et al., *Terrorist Financing: Report of an Independent Task Force Sponsored by the Council of Foreign Relations.* New York: Council of Foreign Relations, 2002. This is a report of the council's findings when evaluating the effectiveness of U.S. efforts to disrupt terrorist financing.

Periodicals

Robert Block and Daniel Pearl, "Underground Trade: Much-Smuggled Gem Called Tanzanite Helps Bin Laden Supporters," *Wall Street Journal,* November 16, 2001.

Asthon Carter, John Deutch, and Philip Zelikow, "Catastrophic Terrorism: Tackling the New Danger," *Foreign Affairs,* November/December 1998.

Stephen Cass, "Listening In: Are the Glory Days of Electronic Spying over—or Just Beginning?" *IEEE Spectrum,* April 2003.

Paul J. Smith, "Transnational Terrorism and the al Qaeda Model: Confronting New Realities," *Parameters,* Summer 2002.

Timothy Thomas, "Al Qaeda and the Internet: The Danger of 'Cyberplanning,'" *Parameters,* Spring 2003.

Paul Wallich, "Getting the Message: It Ain't Just What You Say, It's the Way You Say It," *IEEE Spectrum,* April 2003.

Bob Woodward, "President Broadens Anti-Hussein Order," *Washington Post,* June 16, 2002.

———, "Secret CIA Units Playing a Central Combat Role," *Washington Post,* November 18, 2001.

Internet Sources

ABCNews.com, "New Threats: U.S. Urged to Remain on High Alert," December 3, 2001. www.ABCNews.com.

Greg Barber, "Homeland Security Advisory System." www.pbs.org.

Osama bin Laden, "*Jihad* Against the Jews and Crusaders: World Islamic Front Statement," February 23, 1998. www.fas.org.

Eliot Borin, "Feds Open 'Total' Tech Spy System," *Wired,* August 7, 2002. www.wired.com.

David Brooks, "The Elephantiasis of Reason," *Atlantic Monthly,* January/February 2003. www.theatlantic.com.

Stephen Budiansky, "Losing the Code War: The Great Age of Code Breaking Is over—and with It Much of Our Ability to Track the Communications of Our Enemies," *Atlantic Monthly,* February 2002. www.theatlantic.com.

CNN, "Agent: 'Moussaoui could fly . . . into the WTC,'" May 14, 2002. www.cnn.com.

———, "Ashcroft: New Terror Attack Possible," October 29, 2001. www.cnn.com.

———, "Target Terrorism: The Investigation Continues; Intelligence Community Retraces Its Steps; How Can Attacks Be Prevented?" aired October 6, 2001. Excerpted transcript available at www.cia.gov.

Carl Conetta, "Dislocating Alcyoneus: How to Combat al-Qaeda and the New Terrorism" (Project on Defense Alternatives Briefing Memo #23), June 25, 2002. www.comw.org/pda.

Defense Advanced Research Projects Agency's Website. www.darpa.mil.

Electronic Frontier Foundation, "EFF Analysis of the Provisions of the USA PATRIOT Act That Relate to Online Activities," October 31, 2001. www.eff.org.

Reuel Marc Gerecht, "The Counterterrorist Myth: A Former CIA Operative Explains Why the Terrorist Usama bin Ladin Has Little to Fear from American Intelligence," *Atlantic Monthly,* July/August 2001. www.theatlantic.com.

Suleiman Abu Gheith, "In the Shadow of the Lances," (reprint). www.memri.org.

Paul Harris, John Hooper, and Ed Helmore, "Suddenly, He Was Gone," *Observer,* December 23, 2001. www.observer.co.uk.

Kevin Hogan, "Will Spyware Work?" *Technology Review*, December 2001. www.globalsecurity.org.

Reyko Huang, "Terror Alerts: The Homeland Security Advisory System," April 22, 2002. www.cdi.org.

Charles C. Mann, "Homeland Insecurity: A Top Expert Says America's Approach to Protecting Itself Will Only Make Matters Worse, Forget 'Foolproof' Technology—We Need Systems Designed to Fail Smartly," *Atlantic Monthly*, September 2002. www.theatlantic.com.

Jeanne Meserve and Mike Ahlers, "Terror Threat Lowered to Yellow," April 16, 2003. www.cnn.com.

Judith Miller, Jeff Gerth, and Don Van Natta Jr., "Missed Signals: Many Say U.S. Planned for Terror but Failed to Take Action," *New York Times*, December 30, 2001. www.nytimes.com.

NewsHour with Jim Lehrer, "Liberty vs. Security," September 10, 2002. www.pbs.org.

———, "The Patriot Act," February 12, 2003. www.pbs.org.

———, "Terror Alert," February 7, 2003. www.pbs.org.

NewsMax.com Wires, "Govt. Launches Operation to Deny Terrorists Financing," October 26, 2001. www.NewsMax.com.

Judy Nichols, "Arizona May Ignore Next Orange Alert," *Arizona Republic*, June 1, 2003. www.azcentral.com.

Office of the Press Secretary, "Homeland Security Presidential Directive-3." www.whitehouse.gov.

Aris A. Pappas and James M. Simon Jr., "Daunting Challenges, Hard Decisions: The Intelligence Community, 2001–2015. www.cia.gov.

Al-Qaeda Training Manual. www.usdoj.com.

Belinda Rhodes, "Al-Qaeda's Continuing Threat," March 11, 2002. http://news.bbc.co.uk.

Brian Ross, "Hunting Bin Laden: Delta Force Has Been Practicing in Afghanistan Since 1998, Says Author," September 27, 2001. www.ABCNews.com.

David J. Rothkopf, "Business Versus Terrorism," *Foreign Policy*, May/June 2002. www.foreignpolicy.com.

Colin Soloway, Rod Nordland and Barbie Nadeau, "Hiding (and Seeking) Messages on the Web," *Newsweek*, June 17, 2002. www.freelists.org.

Elsa M. Wenzel, "FBI Computers Enter the 21st Century," *PC World*, April 3, 2003. www.pcworld.com.

Wired, "Total Info System Totally Touchy," December 2, 2002. www.wired.com.

World Policy Institute, "Afghanistan Continued: Does War Really Work?" December 6, 2001. www.worldpolicy.org.

Index

Picture Credits

Cover Photo: © Reuters NewMedia Inc./CORBIS

© AFP/CORBIS, 18, 21, 72, 74, 75, 78, 84

© AP/World Wide Photos, 12, 15, 17, 22, 24, 25, 27, 28, 31, 34, 37, 40, 43, 44, 46, 47, 51, 52, 54, 55, 58, 60, 61, 62, 64, 68, 69, 71, 81, 87, 88, 90, 91

© Collier Photos Bob/CORBIS Sygma, 36

© Reuters NewMedia Inc./CORBIS, 11, 82, 85

© Robert Essel NYC/CORBIS, 16

About the Author

Jennifer Keeley is a freelance writer and former teacher who lives and works in Seattle, Washington. She graduated from Carleton College in 1996 with a degree in history and her teaching certificate. She has taught history and social studies in both the Seattle and Minneapolis public schools.